Caterpillars or Butterflies

Caterpillars or Butterflies

Jane McWhorter

QUALITY PUBLICATIONS
P.O. BOX 7385
FT. WORTH, TX 76111

ACKNOWLEDGMENTS

Excerpt reprinted from THE PROPHET, by Kahlil Gibran, with permission of the publisher, Alfred A. Knopf, Inc. Copyright 1923 by Kahlil Gibran; renewal copyright 1951 by Administrators C.T.A. of Kahlil Gibran Estate, and Mary G. Gibran.

ISBN: 0-89137-410-8

Dedicated with love to Don, by whose side I find my greatest sense of happiness and fulfillment.

Jane McWhorter

TABLE OF CONTENTS

INTRODUCTION

This book has been written with the prayer that it might be of some benefit in helping Christians develop more Christlike temperaments. Conversion is a lifetime process. True, we set our feet on the right path when we become children of God; but obeying the gospel is only the beginning of a new life.

The Bible truly becomes "sweeter as the years go by." The more we meditate upon it, the more clearly all the Scriptures complement one another. I had often read the passage in Galatians 5:22, 23, which depicts the fruit of the Spirit. It has only been in recent years, however, that I happened to fit the parts of the puzzle together and realize that Philippians 4:8 is the answer to Galatians 5:22, 23. A better understanding of these three verses became the goal of my personal Bible study for about a year as I tried to learn all that I could about the meanings of the six thoughts which Christians are to plant in their minds and the nine parts of the resulting fruit of the Spirit. I make no claim to scholarship but have simply used reference books available to every Christian. Since this study has helped me tremendously, I would like to share it with others to be used as the basis for class work or as a guide for daily individual study. Survey courses have their place in the proper development of a child of God. The study of an entire book of the Scriptures also has its merit. Occasionally, however, it is refreshing to delve into just a few verses to discover the various nuances of meaning. As a soft rain slowly soaks into the soil, may these three verses penetrate your thinking.

CATERPILLARS OR BUTTERFLIES

Would I shock you if I ventured to ask whether your Christian life more closely resembles the characteristics of a **caterpillar** or a **butterfly?** If you'll thumb back through the pages of your memory to school days, you probably will recall studying the metamorphosis of an ugly, slimy caterpillar into a beautiful butterfly. Slowly this repulsive creature changes into one of the most delightful of God's handiworks as it emerges from the chrysalis stage. A struggle is a necessary part of this metamorphosis. In experiments scientists have slit the hardened exterior of the pupa to aid the imprisoned creature in its exit. Alas, the butterfly's wings were so weak that it was unable to fly. The struggle to free itself was necessary for proper development.

CHRISTIAN CHARACTER—A TRANSFORMATION

It seems that we have a number of baptized caterpillars crawling about in the church but few truly transformed lives that depict the beauty that God's Word promises. The existence of a butterfly is not possible without the caterpillar stage, but most of us are too content with remaining in this beginning phase. Too many desire the benefits of mature Christianity without being willing to endure its inherent growing pains. We accept God's terms of salvation and become His children through baptism, but we stop at the first rung in our ladder of growth. I'm afraid our friends and neighbors sometimes see us as dogmatic defenders of the first principles of the gospel (as necessary as that is); but they also view our temperaments as cross, selfish, unmerciful and pessimistic. We're going to have a difficult time convincing the people of the world that Christianity is the most desired life when they see the thorns of the Devil instead of the fruit of the Spirit in our lives.

The health department is not alone in innoculating people. It seems that sometimes the Devil uses this same method. A small amount of injected smallpox germs will produce a light case of the dreaded disease and allow our bodies to develop a defense against a real attack. In the same way, new converts sometimes receive only a smattering of Christianity and somehow manage to build up a tremendous resistance to the real thing. Christ means **nothing** in our lives until He is **everything.**

Conversion is a gradual process. Turning from sin and accepting baptism is only the beginning, not the final, stage in our salvation. During the years before the crucifixion Peter followed the Lord more faithfully than most of us would have, yet Christ told this apostle: "But I have prayed for thee, that thy faith fail not: and **when thou art converted,** strengthen thy brethren" (Luke 22:32). Slowly the impetuous fisherman changed into one of the pillars of the church (Galatians 2:9). Romans 12:2 gives the key to this metamorphosis of a Christian: "And be not conformed to this world, but be ye **transformed by the renewing of your mind,** that ye may prove what is that good, and acceptable, and perfect, will of God." "Be renewed in the spirit of your mind" (Ephesians 4:23). Our minds are renewed, or changed, and the result is a transformed personality. This transformation may require years. We Americans suffer an **instant complex.** We're accustomed to our instant coffee, instant hot cereals and so many convenience foods that this impatience extends to almost every facet of our lives. It requires only a short time to **intellectually** learn Bible truths but the **application** may be a lifelong effort. Far too many Christians become frustrated and quit trying.

The first verse of the twelfth chapter of Romans presents the greatest challenge ever offered mankind: "I beseech you therefore, brethren, by the mercies of God, **that ye present your bodies a living sacrifice . . .**" When I was much younger, I used to think that the early Christians who were fed to the lions were the epitome of devotion to the cause of Christ. I'll have to admit that shivers ran up and down my spine when I viewed the Colosseum in Rome and thought of the bravery of those early disciples who chose death rather than deny their beliefs. (I wondered whether or not I would have been so faithful.) Since that time I have realized more and more that a lifetime of devotion to Christ demands just as much sacrifice, if not more, as the momentary summoning of supreme courage for a few hours. Paul admonished the Christians at Rome, the center of torture and barbarian death, not to offer their bodies to the lions but rather to present a **lifetime** of service to prove their devotion. This apostle emphasized the same thought in his epistle to the Galatians: "But God forbid that I should glory, save in the cross of our Lord Jesus Christ, **by whom the world is crucified unto me, and I unto the world**" (Galatians 6:14).

TRANSFORMED BY BEHOLDING CHRIST

Years ago, in my childhood I read Nathaniel Hawthorne's classic story, "The Great Stone Face," which made an indelible impression upon my memory. A certain hamlet was graced by a stone cliff which bore the resemblance of a man. The folklore of the townspeople prophesied the arrival of a man whose countenance would resemble the Great Stone Face. Ernest, a young boy of the town, grew up in these surroundings and anxiously awaited the fulfillment of this promise. Eminent men came to the town—a merchant, a soldier, a statesman and a poet. The local people hoped each would bear a resemblance to the Great Stone Face. One by one their hopes were aborted. Ernest, who had become the sage of the town when he grew to maturity, also felt the disappointment over the lack of fulfillment of this prophecy as he gazed day after day at the stone visage on the mountainside. One day a visitor to the community happened to notice that it was Earnest who bore the resemblance to the Great Stone Face. Years of gazing lovingly at the image on the mountainside had transformed Ernest's face into the same features.

Nathaniel Hawthorne's story is fictitious, but the apostle Paul told the Corinthians about a spiritual transformation that is quite real. In 2 Corinthians 3:18 the writer says: "But **we all,** with **open face** beholding as in a glass the glory of the Lord, **are changed into the same image** from glory to glory, even as by the Spirit of the Lord." The words are not addressed to a chosen few but to all who are willing to comply with the conditions. Notice that an **open face** is necessary—a complete submission to God's will. Just as one might lovingly behold an image in a glass day after day until he gradually assumes the same appearance, even so a Christian is changed into the likeness of Christ by devotedly gazing upon His image. Looking upon the physical appearance of the Lord is not intimated in the passage under consideration. The writer of this verse was permitted to witness the resurrected Christ as a qualification of apostleship, but even this miraculous manifestation was not enough. Paul was told to enter the city of Damascus, where he would be **told** what he must do to be saved (Acts 9:6). We are **told** what we must do through His Word, and it is through this perfect law of liberty that we behold the image necessary for our transformation.

Change from the Inside—Christians know that certain emotions are not Christ-like, but to suppress these feelings from without is much like putting a tight lid on a pan of boiling water: an explosion is inevitable. Modern psychology shows the inherent dangers of bottling up our feelings, which are like artesian wells and must gush freely. There must be a balance, however, between emotional control and emotional expression. Instead of angry diatribes which only hurt the feelings of others, Christians need to learn to express their frustrations and resentments in legitimate outlets. If these feelings are actually within us, they must be channeled and disciplined. Talking over our vexations with God is one outlet. Being able to express how we honestly feel to a trustworthy friend is also a wonderful catharsis. Physical exercise and work constitute good therapy. Instead of repressing antisocial impulses, we can conquer best by acknowledging and facing them. Sweeping undesirable feelings under the rug only makes it lumpy. Often putting fears into words helps them evaporate like steam from a teakettle. Try writing your grievances on paper and then burning them. Once we pull our feelings from the shadows of the subconscious into the light of conscious thoughts, it is much easier to evaluate them properly. When our wrongs have been forgiven by God, we fare much better if we can **renounce**, not **repress**, these past actions and feelings by closing the door upon them. We are not perfect now and we never will be. We need not set standards for ourselves that only a deity could expect to follow, but we **can** become **better** than what we are at the present time. The following saying has been one of my favorites for some time.

"What we **are** is **God's** gift to **us**.
What we **become** is **our** gift to **God**."

The true secret is not to **suppress** the adverse characteristics in our personalities from without but to **prevent** their formation from within. It's not difficult to suppress something that does not exist. Instead of trying to **control** a nasty temper, isn't it better if we can learn not to become vexed over trivial annoyances? Such control is not a natural characteristic and is contrary to human nature. Only when we realize that our sufficiency is of God (2 Corinthians 3:5), can we begin to master our emotions. "He that ruleth his spirit (is better) than he that taketh a city" (Proverbs 16:32). When we fill our minds with the thoughts of our Master, then are we changed into His image: "Christ in you, the hope of glory" (Colossians 1:27). Paul admonished the Philippians: "Let this mind be in you, which was also in Christ Jesus" (Philippians 2:5). Peter told Christians that they could be given "things that pertain unto life and godliness, **through the knowledge of him** that hath called us to glory and virtue" (2 Peter 1:3). Thoughts make the real person. "As he thinketh in his heart, so is he" (Proverbs 23:7). Williams James, the father of American psychology, voiced this same thought when he said, "The greatest discovery of my generation is that human beings can alter their lives by altering their attitudes of mind."

First Step Not Enough—It is absolutely essential for a Christian to give a "Thus saith the Lord" for what he believes and practices. We have learned always to be ready to give an answer (1 Peter 3:15). This is a necessary first step, but I'm afraid too many have become so legalistic that they have overlooked the spirit of the law. Paul warned of following only the letter of God's Word: "Who also hath made us able ministers of the new testament; **not of the letter, but of the spirit;** for the **letter killeth** but the **spirit giveth life"** (2 Corinthians 3:6). Too many of us have just enough Christianity to kill the desire of others to follow. Our lives should display the essence of what true Christianity really offers. **"Ye** are our **epistle** written in **our hearts, known and read of all men"** (2 Corinthians 3:2). How do our lives read to our neighbors?

Suggestions for Class Use

Lesson One

1. Assign one class member the task of doing some research concerning the metamorphosis of a caterpillar to a butterfly, using pictures and drawings to illustrate.
2. What are the first principles involved in becoming a child of God? What qualities should a mature Christian possess? How much growth have you made since your baptism?
3. Peter, who had been a follower of the Lord for nearly three years, was told to strengthen his brethren when he was converted (Luke 22:32). When did Peter become converted? Are we ever fully converted?
4. In the preceding verse (Luke 22:31), Christ observed that Satan desired to have Peter that he might be sifted as wheat. What is the value of Satan's sifting in our lives? Are we still lumpy Christians?
5. How do these passages support the theory that the maturing of a Christian is a gradual process and must go through certain logical stages: (a) Mark 4:28 (b) 1 Peter 2:2 (c) 1 Corinthians 3:1, 2 (d) Hebrews 5:12-14 (e) James 5:7? (The last passage refers to the Lord's coming but the principle of patience is applicable.)
6. According to Romans 12:2, how are we transformed?

7. Do a little research on the tortuous deaths of Christians in the Roman Colosseum, using pictures to illustrate the setting. Which do **you** think calls for more courage: being fed to the lions or living a life of faithful service in everyday trials? Discuss.

8. Have one class member briefly relate the story of "The Great Stone Face."

9. How are we changed into the image of the Lord? (See 2 Corinthians 3:18).

10. Why is it best not to simply suppress adverse characteristics in our personalities? What are some legitimate outlets for these feelings? What is a better means of control?

11. According to Proverbs 23:7, what determines the true personality of a person?

12. In 2 Corinthians 3:6 we are told that the letter of the law killeth. Illustrate from real life situations how a legalistic approach to the Word can kill any desire for others to be converted when the right attitude is missing. Do some research on the legalistic approach of the Pharisees.

13. How are we epistles to be read of all men? (See 2 Corinthians 3:2).

THE ANSWER

A number of Scriptures urge Christians to become more Christ-like. "Whereby are given unto us exceeding great and precious promises; that by these ye might be **partakers of the divine nature**" (2 Peter 1:4). Ephesians 4:13 admonishes us to become full-grown "unto the measure of the stature of the **fulness of Christ.**" "Forasmuch then as Christ hath suffered for us in the flesh, arm yourselves likewise with the **same mind**" (1 Peter 4:1). When we speak of being transformed into the image of Christ and partakers of the divine nature, perhaps it would be wise to clarify the true nature of Christ. Often too many think of the Master as an emotionless zombie, but this Galilean displayed **strong** emotions.

A CONTRAST

The sins of Jerusalem brought tears to the eyes of Christ as He wept over the inhabitants of His beloved city. The sorrow accompanying the death of a dear friend prompted this same display of emotion (John 11:35). Not only did our Lord experience sorrow, but he also knew anger. Notice how His anger differed from ours: **Christ became angry when men failed to obey God.** He became so angry with the money changers that He drove them from the temple (John 2:13-16). When the Jews rebuked Jesus for healing the withered hand on the Sabbath, He was so vexed over the hardness of their hearts in failing to see the real spirit of the law that He "looked round about on them with anger" (Mark 3:5). In contrast, **when we see men disobeying God, our attitude is that of complacency—not anger.** We do not call them sinners. We say they have emotional problems. Contrast the cause of Christ's anger with the basis for our flare-ups. A person can disobey God all he likes and we make excuses. Let him insult us, however, and we are ready to lash out with our tongues. Although we usually become angry over personal insult, Christ accepted this type of injustice without anger. When you have time, thoughtfully read the accounts of the trial and death of our Lord. He accepted spitting in His face, slapping and mockery of His deity. He even refused to answer their accusations. When His beloved friend, Peter, denied Him, the only rebuke Christ displayed must have been in His eyes for "the Lord turned, and looked upon Peter." That look probably was filled with hurt and disappointment, not anger, because Peter went out and wept bitterly (Luke 22:61, 62).

In summary we might say that instead of becoming angry with sin as did Christ, we tend to placate transgressions. When **our** feelings become hurt, however, and our toes are stepped upon, we pout with the smugness of Jonah as we justify our actions: "I do well to be angry" (Jonah 4:9). There is justifiable reason for anger—a right way to be angry. "Be ye angry, and sin not" (Ephesians 4:26). Let us become indignant over sin against God, not injustices toward ourselves.

THE SOLUTION

Have you ever become discouraged when you have compared your life with the divine characteristics of a godly life? I have. Read again Galatians 5:22, 23: "But the fruit of the Spirit is love, joy, peace, long-suffering, gentleness, goodness, faith, meekness, temperance: against such there is no law." We know the identifying marks of a true Christian; and we try to suppress our tempers, our irritability, our impatience. Such attempts are comparable to sealing a pot of boiling water. The control must come, not from the outside, but from within. God gives the answer to this enigma in Philippians 4:8: "Finally, brethren, whatsoever things are true, whatsoever things are honest, whatsoever things are just, whatsoever things are pure, whatsoever things are lovely, whatsoever things are of good report; if there be any virtue, and if there be any praise, think on these things." These are the seeds we **must** plant in our minds if we expect to harvest the fruit of Galatians 5:22, 23. Thoughts that are true, honest, just, pure, lovely and of good report **will** produce the characteristics of love, joy, peace, longsuffering, gentleness, goodness, faith, meekness and temperance. A similar list of Christian characteristics is given in the first chapter of 2 Peter: "For if these things be in you, and abound, they make you that ye shall **neither be barren nor unfruitful** in the knowledge of our Lord Jesus Christ" (2 Peter 1:8). These attitudes are not something we diligently work upon. Instead, they are byproducts of the right seeds. A fruit is not produced by itself but is the result of something else. We desire the fruit without the bother of planting and cultivating. "Whatsoever a man soweth, that shall he also reap" (Galatians 6:7). "Ye are God's husbandry" (1 Corinthians 3:9). "For a good tree bringeth not forth corrupt fruit; neither doth a corrupt tree bring forth good fruit. For every tree is known by his own fruit" (Luke 6:43, 44). "Can the fig tree, my brethren, bear olive berries? either a vine, figs?" (James 3:12). "Wherefore by their fruits ye shall know them" (Matthew 7:20). Christians are told to be "filled with the fruits of righteousness" (Philippians 1:11). Paul told the Colossians that they should be fruitful in every good work (Colossians 1:10).

WRONG APPROACH

Our trouble is this: we plant turnip seeds in our minds, allow dandelions to blow in and then wonder why we don't have a rose garden. When we plant and cultivate the **right** seed, the **right** fruit will be produced. **This is God's answer to the transformation of a Christian's mind.** Most of us wonder why we are not transformed into persons of better temperaments. We **could** become butterflies, but we're not willing to undergo the struggle necessary to change a caterpillar into a butterfly. Someone has said: "A woman deserves no credit for her beauty at sixteen but beauty at sixty is her soul's doing."

A CONTINUAL THOUGHT PROCESS

Our minds are the soil in which the seeds of our thoughts grow. "Chance only favors the mind which is prepared" (Louis Pasteur). We cannot think about things that are true, honest, just, pure, lovely and of good report one hour a week or even one hour a day and expect to flutter like butterflies. Just as we are to pray without ceasing, so must our thoughts be constantly focused upon the right seeds.

Emerson observed: "A man **is** what he **thinks** about all day long." Long ago Plato stated the same thought when he said: "We become what we contemplate." Sir Isaac Newton was the object of mockery by his neighbors because he spent hours blowing soap bubbles in his garden. Years later, when he was asked how he discovered the principle of gravitation, he replied, "By thinking about it all the time." Newton also offered this explanation of his success: "If I have made any improvement in the sciences, it is owing more to patient attention than to anything else." Just as Newton thought about the soap bubbles as he went about his other tasks, so must we constantly fill our minds with the right thoughts. We should train our subconscious thoughts to think about these things even when our conscious thought processes are busy with other ideas. Too many Christians take the Word of God just as they do bad-tasting medicine. They tolerate it when they **have** to do so just to get it over with and out of the way. They have never known the delight that the psalmist experienced as he meditated upon the Law of God day and night (Psalms 1:2).

Suggestions for Class Use

Lesson Two

1. Relate two instances in which Christ shed tears.
2. Our Lord also knew anger. Discuss such occasions.

3. On the chalkboard or overhead projector compile a list of the injustices Jesus endured during His trial and death. (See Matthew 27, Mark 15, Luke 23, John 18 and 19.)
4. Read aloud the account of Peter's denial (Luke 22:54-62). Try to stand in Peter's shoes as his eyes met the look of Christ. Peter remembered the Word of the Lord and wept Discuss the importance of planting the Word of God in our hearts so that we might remember in times of trial and temptation.
5. Contrast the cause of Christ's anger with the basis for most of our flare-ups.
6. Why is there a positive command to be angry? (Ephesians 4:26)
7. Divide the class into six groups and allow a few minutes for off-the-cuff definitions of the proper thoughts mentioned in Philippians 4:8.
8. Follow the same procedure for the fruit of the Spirit discussed in Galatians 5:22, 23. Let a spokesman for each group report to the class.
9. As each group gives an account of its work, on the chalkboard illustrate the necessary seed falling into the ground and producing the right fruit as God's answer to the transformation of a Christian's mind.
10. Discuss the idea of the term "**fruit** instead of **fruits** in Galatians 5:22 as a composite of the various parts. Isn't a Christian's life a blending of all the fruits into one whole?
11. Compare the characteristics of a Christian in Galatians 5:22, 23 with those in 2 Peter 1:5, 8.
12. Have buzz groups to discover ways to train our minds to think subconsciously about the right thoughts. How can we think about something when we're not even conscious that it's on our minds?
13. Do you agree or disagree with the statement of William James: "The greatest discovery of my generation is that we can alter our lives by altering our attitude of mind"?
14. Examine Psalm 119:97 and Psalm 1:2 and relate to question eleven.
15. How can you reconcile the statement that David was a man of God's own heart with the grievous sins of this great king?

NO NEW THING UNDER THE SUN

Far too often man becomes inflated over ideas of his own importance. He gloats over new discoveries while failing to realize that the basic principles upon which his work is based have been known for years. Centuries ago the wise writer of Ecclesiastes observed: "There is no new thing under the sun. Is there any thing whereof it may be said, See this is new? it hath been already of old time, which was before us" (Ecclesiastes 1:9, 10).

RECENT FINDINGS

More than eighteen hundred years ago Marcus Aurelius, the Roman emperor, observed. "Our life is what our thoughts make it." Centuries later John Milton said: "The mind is its own place, and in itself can make a heaven of Hell, a hell of Heaven." During this century many studies of the human mind and its functions have been made. Let's consider some of these philosophies and then see how they correlate with the Word of God.

The mind has two parts, each functioning differently. The **conscious** part of the brain does the rational thinking and possesses the deep desires, both of which are equally important. It is this part of the mind which sets our lifetime goals. If they are too high, frustration is inevitable. If they are too low, very little will ever be achieved. Humans are, by nature, goal-seeking individuals. We do our best work when striving to reach a desired image. In fact, defending the status quo, or feeling that we have arrived, causes us to become static. In setting lifetime goals the conscious part of the mind poses the problems which will have to be overcome. It also controls the information entering the brain; and, in so doing, motivates the subconscious by suggestion, repetition, and expectancy. Like a master architect the conscious draws the plans and then hands the actual building details over to the subconscious.

Working constantly, the **subconscious** part of the mind functions in a different manner from the conscious. It is this part of the brain which has inspiration, imagination and memory. Much as a computer solves its problems or a missile follows its course toward a target, the subconscious reacts automatically to the information given it by the conscious and the course upon which it has been set. The nature of these two factors is instrumental in determining whether one is a failure or a success. The conscious part of the mind plants the seed in the soil of the subconscious and provides the proper water and fertilizer for growth.

Goals are **set** by the conscious but it is the subconscious which **strives** toward those goals. It is just as difficult for a tightrope walker to maintain his balance while standing still as it is to live successfully a life without goals. Such a life is similar to a ship that leaves port without a destination or a definite way of getting there. Goals may be good or bad. If a person sees himself as a failure in life and that is the goal or image toward which he is striving, then the subconscious will believe that **this** is the direction toward which it is aiming. Our ultimate happiness and sense of worth, therefore, depend upon the **kind** of goal toward which we are reaching. Goals based upon status symbols or trying to win the approval of others can never be desirable ones. Naturally, if the image which we hold of ourselves is a negative one, then the subconscious will direct the course of our lives in that direction. Like a magnet, the mind will find that for which it is looking.

Even when the conscious part of the mind has set desirable lifetime goals, we should not be discouraged over temporary

failures. Mistakes can be steppingstones to success. Just as a missile has negative feedback or failures and corrects its course accordingly, so does the healthy subconscious regard failures only as temporary obstacles in its course to the goal. Failure, like success, is one of the great experiences of life and is a part of the learning process. Accomplishment is a natural result of trial and error. Mistakes should be analyzed, used beneficially for any inherent lesson, and then be forgotten when they have served their purpose. Used intelligently, the past tells us how we reached our present status and helps us understand why we act as we do now. To constantly **dwell** upon past failures and humiliations can hypnotize us into thinking we can't be any better. Fear of failure is a form of self-suicide. Too many suffocate themselves with self-concern and could say with Dickens: "I wear the chain I forged in life." When we stop giving utmost importance to the past, it begins to lose its negative power over us. Remember, no race was run by looking backward.

Contrary to the theories depicting man as a helpless victim of his past, recent studies have shown that the mature person can analyze his past to help him understand his present attitudes and then use his mature thinking to direct his course in the direction toward which he wants to go. There is a vast difference between **repression** and **renunciation.** Repression usually leads to more trouble, whereas renunciation implies a mature rejection of past mistakes which cannot be corrected or used beneficially. A great deal of our subconscious thoughts are based upon the unquestioned teachings of our parents during the first few years of our lives. Another segment relates to our childhood **feelings** about life. Both influence the way we react as adults. It requires a mature person to analyze these two factors of subconscious thinking and either accept or reject them upon the basis of what is actually true for the adult. The past tells us **how** we got to the present point of our lives. What we **do** in the future is our own responsibility. We can either continually dwell upon broken records of unhappy earlier experiences until they smother our ambitions like quicksand or we can put on a new record and change the tune of our lives. Although we can't change the past, we can change the meaning. Instead of dwelling on **past mistakes,** we should remember our successful efforts as the best way to accomplish what we desire. Although it is unwise to dwell upon errors of the past, we must realize that we have to be willing to make **some** mistakes if we are to succeed in life. Someone has said that **triumph** is just **umph** added to **try.** "Footprints in the sands of time were not made by sitting down." Everyone knows that the only time a turtle ever makes any progress is when it sticks its neck out. Most people who have succeeded in a worldly sense have also made many failures. Studies have shown that people who are successful in various fields have a common trait—persistence. They keep on trying when most people would have given up. Someone once observed that diamonds are pieces of coal that stuck to their jobs. "Great works are performed, not by strength, but by perseverance" (Samuel Johnson). Look at Abraham Lincoln. A year after failing in business, he was defeated in a state election. Two years later he suffered another business failure. Nine more years brought another election defeat. Eleven years after that, he lost agian. Another four years saw one more loss at the polls. But persistence paid off. Two years after the last loss, Abraham Lincoln became President.

Robert Frost, four-time winner of the Pulitzer Prize for poetry and the author of literary works which have been published in 22 languages, could have been considered a failure for 20 years. Perseverance paid off for this great American poet who was 39 years old before he ever sold a volume of poetry. Winston Churchill was jailed during the Boer War in Pretoria, South Africa. Later when he became first lord of the admiralty, he was blamed for the Dardanelles disaster and forced to resign. After he had seen his nation successfully through another war, he was rejected at the polls. From this he rose to become Prime Minister of Great Britain and the most esteemed man of his generation. Thomas Edison made many, many mistakes in his inventions but simply regarded them as methods which would not work. The automobile, the radio, the telephone—all were the result of many mistakes. Babe Ruth, who led the American League in home runs for 12 years and was regarded as the "Home Run King," also held the record for the most strikeouts. If the fear of striking out had caused him to refuse to try, this baseball hero would never have been a success. Many machines have negative signals on them to inform the operators when something has gone wrong, but we don't throw a machine away just because it has these negative aspects. When a negative signal flashes, the operator corrects the mistake and then proceeds on his course.

Theodore Roosevelt has the right idea when he said, "Far better it is to dare mighty things, to win glorious triumphs, even checkered by failure, than to take rank with those poor spirits who neither enjoy much nor suffer because they live in the gray twilight that knows neither victory nor defeat."

Studies have shown the importance of the **mental picture** which the subconscious holds. "A man's life is dyed by the color of his imagination" (Marcus Aurelius). Whether the idea is true or not, the subconscious will react according to what it **believes** to be true. For example, saliva glands in the mouths of humans can be activated by the mental picture of delicious food. In the famous experiment with Pavlov's dogs, the animals heard a bell, then received food. Next the bell was sounded without the reward of food. This was repeated many times. The animals' physical reflexes had been so conditioned that they learned to salivate at the sound of the bell without being fed. The same principle works on the human level in hypnosis. When the subconscious believes that the room is excessively hot, body temperature will actually increase. If the hypnotized person believes that he cannot lift his hand off the table, it becomes virtually impossible. A person does not have to confront a live snake across his path to cause him to run. A prankster may have placed a dead one there. If the subconscious **thinks** the snake is alive, the same amount of adrenalin will flow into the bloodstream to insure a hasty flight as would be released if the snake really were alive. Emotions also determine the dialation or contraction of the small arteries by means of the vasomotor nerves. It is the emotions which make the face flush or turn white. These same emotions trigger many unseen chemical reactions inside the body. The conscious part of the mind **reasons**. The subconscious reacts automatically to what it **believes** to be true.

Willfully trying to break a bad habit simply reinforces it and causes the negative to become the goal. When a person worries about something undesirable that might happen, he repeatedly thinks of the possible result with such vividness that it seems real to the subconscious, which in turn reacts automatically to the information given it and also the goals set by the conscious. The feared outcome seems so real to the subconscious that automatic body functions are triggered to combat the dreaded event. Excessive gastric juices and adrenalin helped our forefathers prepare their bodies to run from Indians and today they help us jump out of the path of an oncoming car. These reactions are totally inappropriate, however, for most of today's problems. The same automatic reactions over a sustained period of time produce ulcers, high blood pressure and many other psychosomatic maladies. "Worry is a thin stream of fear, which, if allowed to trickle through the mind, soon cuts a channel into which all thoughts flow." Worry may begin like a trickle over our subconscious but can easily increase to the intensity of a raging river which consumes all thought until it becomes an obsession.

When we constantly worry about what **might** happen, our body reacts in the same manner as if the dreaded thing were **real.** We can't control our automatic feelings and reactions by will power. Instead, we must substitute good for bad. When we assume that something desirable is possible and constantly dwell upon such thoughts, then the subconscious responds automatically with cheerfulness and happiness. Thus, we should set goals for what we **want,** not what we **don't** want.

Good self-esteem is necessary. Our thoughts affect our feelings, which in turn affect our actions. This helps to explain why some gifted people fail and many average persons succeed. What a person thinks of himself will affect what others think of him. If he doesn't like himself, neither will others. According to studies sponsored by the National Science Foundation, self-acceptance and social acceptance go hand in hand. Sometimes the view of ourselves is so negative that a completely new and different self-image must be planted in the mind of the subconscious. Man will **strive** to be the kind of person he **thinks** it is possible for him to be. We are controlled, to a great degree, by the mental picture we develop of ourselves. It is of utmost importance that we have a vivid idea of the kind of person we hope to become. Such a goal must be adequate and realistic or it will bring frustration. When a person's basic opinion of himself is good and he is realistically striving for betterment, he feels secure and self-confident. Such a person realizes that he makes mistakes along the way, but he had a mental image of the kind of person he is striving to become and corrects his mistakes to set him back on the desired path. Self-confidence comes from small experiences of success, which in turn lead to larger ones. Our opinion of the kind of person we **can** become sets the boundaries of what is possible. Good self-esteem does not create new talents. Instead, it releases dormant ones.

COMPARISON WITH GOD'S WORD

It does not matter how well the various theories of human behavior may be accepted; there is only one real standard of truth—the Word of God (John 17:17). Let's take the potpourri of men's philosophies discussed in the previous section and hold it to the eternal light.

Modern behaviorists are not the first to realize that **a man's actions reflect what he thinks.** The writer of Proverbs said, ". . . for as he thinketh in his heart, so is he" (Proverbs 23:7). "Out of the abundance of the heart the mouth speaketh" (Matthew 12:34). "A good man out of the good treasure of his heart bringeth forth that which is good; and an evil man out of the evil treasure of his heart bringeth forth that which is evil: for of the abundance of the heart his mouth speaketh" (Luke 6:45). Any changing of an individual must begin on the inside. In fact, the only thing over which a person has complete control is his mind. Christ condemned hypocritical religious leaders of His day by calling them whited sepulchres. "Woe unto you, scribes and Pharisees, hypocrites! for ye are like unto whited sepulchres, which indeed appear beautiful outward, but are within full of dead men's bones, and of all uncleanness. Even so ye also outwardly appear righteous unto men, but within ye are full of hypocrisy and iniquity" (Matthew 23:27, 28). It was along this same vein of thought that Paul said: "Finally, brethren, whatsoever things are true, whatsoever things are honest, whatsoever things are just, whatsoever things are pure, whatsoever things are lovely, whatsoever things are of good report; if there be any virtue, and if there be any praise, **think on these things**" (Philippians 4:8).

The conscious must constantly search for thoughts that are pure, wholesome and uplifting to feed to the subconscious. When this is done consistently, some of our best, most creative thoughts can emerge from the subconscious without any conscious effort on our part.

Goals, or aims in life, are found at the core of God's plan of salvation. Too many people dissipate their energy with trivia, worry and fear instead of focusing all efforts toward a major goal. An intense purpose in life actually helps to produce more energy by setting up chemical reactions inside the body. Christians today should have the same meaningful obsession as Paul: "I press toward the mark for the prize of the high calling of God in Christ Jesus" (Philippians 3:14). Neither was this apostle drifting aimlessly through life when he said: "Let us run with patience the race that is set before us" (Hebrews 12:1).

If a person is wise, he will ask for a purpose in life instead of a great talent. Success is dependent not so much upon talent or opportunity as perseverance. Someone once observed that genius is the power of continuous effort. A little extra effort can make the difference between failure and success. When someone knows **where** he is going and has a great desire to get there, his whole being, even his subconscious, will focus all creative talent toward reaching that goal. "He who is firm in will molds the world to himself" (Geothe). An ancient Chinese proverb says: "Great souls have wills; feeble ones have only wishes." It is frequently the mental picture of the person whom he hopes to become that gives the Christian the courage to keep on trying when all effort seems hopeless. Many times he is spared the consequences of doing something wrong, even when pressure is put upon him, because he thinks that he is just not the **kind** of person who would do such a thing. This same mental image also prevents a temporary slip from becoming permanent.

Everyone makes mistakes, but the dedicated Christian is master of his mistakes and uses them to push him closer to becoming the kind of person he hopes to be. Through trial and error he learns the secret of falling forward instead of backward. Anyone who has ever flown across the Atlantic is aware of the effect of the tail winds. The return trip usually requires about an hour longer than the initial flight because the wind is in front of the plane instead of behind it. If we can only learn to fall forward, we can get life's tail wind of mistakes behind us to push us on to greater success. Ralph Waldo Emerson had this same philosophy in mind when he wrote: "Do not be too timid and squeamish about your actions. All life is an experiment. The more experiments you make, the better. What if they are a little coarse, and you may get your coat soiled or torn? What if you do fail, and get fairly rolled in the dirt once or twice? Up again, you shall never be so afraid of a tumble."

I have read that an expert can tell a fine oriental rug from one made commercially by its strange variations of pattern. In the villages where these rugs are produced, a master weaver is in charge of a number of young men who individually weave each rug. Naturally, there will often be some mistakes. The master weaver, instead of pulling the threads out to right the wrong, will find some way to blend the mistakes into the over-all pattern and produce an even more beautiful design than the originally intended one. These rugs are exquisite because someone knows how to turn mistakes into works of art. As children of God, we have a promise not afforded those outside His family: when a wrong has been confessed and everything humanly possible has been done to make restitutions, then we may cease to bear the guilt. Like Paul we may forget those things which are behind (Philippians 3:13). Instead of brooding over mistakes which have already been forgiven, we may use them as steppingstones to become better people. Christians would do well to take a few weaving lessons.

We sometimes get the cart before the horse. Realizing that we have undesirable traits, we do everything within our power to break such habits. Gritting our teeth and resolving with great determination never again to entertain such thoughts often reinforces the habit. By keeping the bad habit constantly in our minds, even when trying to overcome it, the negative becomes a goal. Anything that continually occupies the mind becomes an obsession. Along the same line of thought, worry about what **might** happen tends to steer us in that direction. "Take therefore no thought for the morrow: for the morrow shall take thought for the things of itself" (Matthew 6:34). Verse 33 of the same chapter admonishes us to seek first the kingdom of God instead of worrying about what might happen. Further warnings concerning undue worrying are given in Philippians 4:6: "Be careful for nothing; but in every thing by prayer and supplication with thanksgiving let your requests be made known unto God." It is only when we do all we can and then lay our cares in the hands of God that we can find the peace that passeth all understanding (Philippians 4:7).

The necessity of replacing good thoughts for bad ones is further found in Matthew 12:43-45 in the teaching concerning the unclean spirit which returned to find the house empty, swept and garnished. Just as the evil spirit then returned with seven other spirits more wicked than he, so will our rejected evil thoughts come back with a host of others **unless** good thoughts leave them no room.

We must believe in ourselves. A child of God has a new self-image. Just as it is unwise to sew a new piece of cloth on an old garment or put new wine into old bottles (Matthew 9:16, 17), so it is unwise for a Christian to try to patch up his old, battle-scarred life. Instead, he is a new creature. "Therefore if any man be in Christ, he is a new creature: old things are passed away" (2 Corinthians 5:17). This potential new creature locked up inside each of us can be just as beautiful as a butterfly, but far too many Christians never go to the trouble. Content to crawl around like caterpillars, such people never seem to realize that man was made a little lower than the angels (Psalms 8:5). Like the one-talent man who hid his little treasure in the earth (Matthew 25:24, 25), Christians who are content to remain as caterpillars fail to use whatever ability they might possess simply because they are unwilling to

try. "The reason most men do not achieve more is because they do not attempt more." Just as a flower seed does not become beautiful until it breaks out of itself and produces the lovely blossom, neither can we reach our God-given potentialities until we break out of our shells. "If we did all the things we are capable of doing, we would literally astound ourselves" (Thomas A. Edison). "Self-trust is the first secret of success" (Ralph Waldo Emerson).

The lessons that follow will deal with the practical applications of unlocking our potentialities, or producing the fruit of Galatians 5:22, 23 by planting the right seeds (thoughts) constantly in our minds (Philippians 4:8). Thinking the right thoughts is the only way we can be changed into the creatures which God would have us be.

Whatsoever things are true, honest, just, pure, lovely and of good report, think on these things.

Suggestions for Class Use

Lesson Three

1. What did the writer of Ecclesiastes mean when he said: "There is no new thing under the sun"?
2. Do you agree with Marcus Aurelius that our life is what our thoughts make it or with the philosophy that man is a victim of circumstances?
3. A week before class assign two people the task of presenting the functions of the two parts of the mind.
4. Which part of the mind sets goals? Which part strives toward those goals? Why are the right goals so important?
5. How should the healthy mind regard temporary failures? Cite examples of both good and bad uses of failures. How can mistakes be a part of the learning process and help us become better?
6. In what sense does the subconscious react according to what it believes to be true? How do the experiments with Pavlov's dogs and with hypnosis support this theory?
7. How can willfully trying to break a bad habit serve to reinforce it?
8. Give examples of physical maladies produced when a

person believes something undesirable might happen. Is there any physical difference in our reactions to either imagined or real dangers?

9. Why should we set goals for what we **want** instead of what we **don't** want?
10. Since most people strive to be the kind of persons they think it is possible for them to be (good or bad), why is good self-esteem necessary?
11. What is the only acceptable standard of truth? (John 17:17)
12. How do actions reflect what a person thinks? (Proverbs 23:7; Matthew 12:34; Luke 6:45; Matthew 23:27, 28)
13. Where must the changing of an individual begin?
14. In what sense did Christ compare the scribes and Pharisees to whited sepulchres?
15. What sort of thoughts did Paul urge the Philippians to think upon? (Philippians 4:8)
16. When pure, wholesome, worthwhile thoughts are constantly fed to the subconscious, what is the result?
17. What was Paul's goal in life? (Philippians 3:14; Hebrews 12:1)
18. Why is a purpose in life more important than a talent?
19. What is the difference in simply falling and in falling forward? Illustrate with the advantage of a tail wind in pushing an airplane forward.
20. What makes a fine oriental rug so exquisite? Apply this to the life of a Christian.
21. How does God promise to regard a Christian's past mistakes?
22. How can mistakes be used to our advantage?
23. Use these passages to prove the folly of worrying about what might happen: Matthew 6:33, 34; Philippians 4:6.
24. In Matthew 12:43-45 what happened to the house that had been the dwelling place of an unclean spirit? Apply this teaching to our thoughts.
25. Why is it necessary for a Christian to become a **new** creature instead of patching up the old one? (Note Ephesians 4:22, 24)
26. Is it egotistical for a Christian to believe in himself? Explain.
27. If we are to produce the fruit of Galatians 5:22, 23, what are the seeds which must be planted?

28. The psalmist said: "Create in me a clean heart, O God; and renew a right spirit within me" (Psalm 51:10). What is our part?

WHATSOEVER THINGS ARE TRUE AND HONEST

It is difficult to pinpoint the meaning of such a nebulous word as **true.** It means so many things to different people. Pilate must have been quite perplexed as Christ informed the ruler: "Everyone that is of the truth heareth my voice" (John 18:37). It was this statement which provoked the inquiry: "What is truth?" (verse 38).

Instead of offering our opinions, let's allow God's Word to interpret itself. **Alethes,** the original Greek word for **true** as it is used in Philippians 4:8, means true to fact, conforming to reality. The same word is used in the following passages:
  (1) Christ said that His record is true (John 8:14).
  (2) All the things which John spoke of Christ were true (John 10:41).
  (3) The record of the one who saw the side of Christ pierced is true (John 19:35).
  (4) The testimony of John concerning Christ is true (John 21:24).
  (5) When Peter was delivered from prison, he "wist not that it was true which was done by the angel; but thought he saw a vision" (Acts 12:9).
  (6) John wrote of a new commandment which was true (1 John 2:8).

38

(7) In his third epistle John spoke of the record as being true (verse 12).

(8) Peter testified of the true grace of God (1 Peter 5:12).

(9) In his second epistle Peter referred to a true proverb (2:22).

(10) In writing Titus Paul said: "This witness is true" (Titus 1:13).

As you read through these verses, you will find that nearly every time the word is used, the passage is referring to a member of the Godhead or an inspired writing. From this study it seems that the connotation of the word has a close affinity to things of a divine nature. Modern philosophers tell us that what is true for you is not necessarily true for me. I suppose this would be an accurate evaluation of man's wisdom, but God's Word is the final authority. It alone is true.

Let's turn from the adjective form of this word (true-alethes) to the noun (truth-aletheia). Note the following: "I am the way, **the truth,** and the life" (John 14:6). "Thy word is **truth**" (John 17:17). When Christ was before Pilate, He said: "To this end was I born, and for this cause came I into the world, that I should bear witness unto **the truth.** Every one that is of **the truth** heareth my voice" (John 18:37). It was then that Pilate asked: "What is **truth**" (verse 38).

TRUE AS IT APPLIES TODAY

In summary, we may say that Christians are to think first of all upon things that are true—thy **word** is truth. More important than anything else, our minds are to be filled with His Word. "Let the word of Christ dwell in you richly in all wisdom" (Colossians 3:16). "Thy word have I hid in mine heart, that I might not sin against thee" (Psalms 119:11). Honestly, how much time do we spend filling our hearts with a study of the Bible? Thirty minutes a **day?** Thirty minutes a **week?** How much time do we spend really **meditating** upon it? It's the first—and most important—step in the transformation of caterpillars into butterflies.

More important than anything else, we are to drop the seeds of God's Word into our minds. We're all busy—too busy for our own good. There is so much that needs to be done each day, things that truly seem necessary. If we are completely honest with ourselves, however, we will find that we devote most of our time to things that are trivial in God's sight. We have so many labor-saving devices that we **ought** to have more spare time than our grandparents. We don't have to devote as much time to the necessities of life: something to eat, a place to sleep and clothes on our backs. So what do we do with our spare time? We either take a job to buy more **things** or we become so involved in various activities that we are exhausted by the end of the day. If we do take a few minutes to read a chapter before retiring, it often becomes only a conscience-easing habit. Somewhere along the line we've missed the real **joy** of meeting our Lord each day through the pages of His Word. "Thy words were found, and I did eat them; and thy word was unto me the joy and rejoicing of mine heart" (Jeremiah 15:16).

Each person has different likes and dislikes. The form of Bible study that appeals to one person may be completely uninteresting to another. Some study by chapters; some prefer topics. Others study by characters. Still others like to supplement a study with reference books. Select a style that appeals to you and **stick with it.** You'll never be caught up with all the routine things you ought to do anyway. Set aside some time each day to study and then **keep the appointment faithfully.**

Too many of us are spasmodic in our studying. We become ashamed and diligently study for awhile, but we all know how difficult it becomes as we are pressed for time. A gully-washing rain isn't good for seeds anyway; they're usually washed away. When a farmer plants his crops, he is interested in frequent, soft rains to provide the proper moisture for the young plants. (Note Deuteronomy 32:2). Proper Bible study, like most habits, has to be initiated by the will until it becomes an established pattern and ingrained in our behavior.

Whatsoever things pertain to the Word of God . . . think on these things.

WORD STUDY OF **HONEST**

When we talk about the word **honest,** everyone nods in agreement over its meaning. **Honest** simply means that we're not dishonest—that we are always truthful in what we do or say. We don't lie. We don't steal. When we do a little searching into translations of the original word (semnos), however, we find different nuances of meaning. **Semnos** means whatever is honorable, grave, decent, nobly serious and venerable (worthy of reverence). This was the word characteristically used to refer to the gods and to the temples of the gods. The word really describes that which has the dignity of holiness upon it.

HONEST IN OUR EVERYDAY LIVES

All these definitions sound a little hazy. Let's nail them down with some concrete illustrations. Be truthful. How many serious, decent thoughts have wandered in and out of our minds today? How many of them are worthy of reverence? How many would we proudly display before the throne of God? A Christian's life was never meant to be one of such solemnity that all joy is absent. Certainly there are times of lightheartedness. (In your concordance, look up the references on rejoicing and joy.) But a Christian should not go through life thinking only of the flippant and cheap. The main stream running through his mind is deep; it is very serious. He is here for a purpose—to prepare himself to go to heaven and take others with him. Everything else is subservient.

Let's check ourselves. What did we think about while we were cooking breakfast? Were our sluggish thoughts only on the bacon and eggs or did we also think about nurturing the spiritual needs of our families? Were we subconsciously planning the day's activities to include something we would be proud to show our Father? What were our thoughts as we vacuumed? Washed dishes? Waited at the traffic light? Sat waiting at the doctor's office? There are so many moments each day when our hands are busy doing rote chores, but our minds are free. Each year we spend hours waiting for appointments. At these times do we ponder some Scripture we've tucked into the recesses of our subconscious? Do we meditate upon the work of the church and the ways we can help? Or do we wonder what will happen next on our favorite soap opera? Do our smoldering thoughts dwell upon real or imagined slights and hurts to our egos?

Whatsoever things are serious, decent and worthy of reverence . . . think on these things.

Suggestions for Class Use

Lesson Four

1. Describe the circumstances under which Christ made the statement: "Everyone that is of the truth heareth my voice" (John 18:37). Why was Pilate so perplexed when he questioned in verse 38: "What is truth?"
2. Read some passages which contain the original Greek word for **true** aloud in class. To what does **true** refer?
3. Compare situation ethics (what is right for you may not be right for me) with the philosophy that the Word of God is the only accurate standard.
4. Give some passages that use the noun form (truth-alethes). To what does this word refer?
5. What are some characteristics of truth? (See John 8:32; Psalm 100:5; Zechariah 8:19; 1 Corinthians 13:6.)
6. If we are to fill our minds with things that are true, what does this mean in everyday language?
7. Contrast the way in which people usually spend a day with the manner in which our grandparents used their time. In reality, have our labor-saving devices given us more time?
8. Divide the class into groups of two or three to discuss ways of making individual Bible study more interesting. Report to the class. Have each class member select a method which appeals to him and write his resolution on a slip of paper. Collect these and ask for results at the end of a month.
9. In the parable of the soils, fruit is produced with **patience** when the seed falls into **honest** and **good** hearts and is **kept** there (Luke 8:15). Comment on the bold face words.
10. Discuss the proper balance between lightheartedness and

seriousness in a Christian's life. Of the two traits, which one should be dominant?

11. We are all creatures of habit and have to be trained to substitute trivial thoughts for those that are suitable to display before the throne of God. Give each class member seven 4 x 6 inch cards. Each day for the next week, ask them to keep a record of their thoughts as they perform routine tasks. At the next class period, begin with a sharing session to compare the results.

WHATSOEVER THINGS ARE JUST AND PURE

I thought I knew the meaning of **just** until I did some "digging" for this study. The original word is **dikaios,** and the Greeks defined the **dikaios** man as one who gives to gods and men that which is their due. It is "duty faced and duty done." In our everyday words, I suppose we could say that it is doing our duty toward God and toward man. These words are still vague, so let's look at some concrete examples.

BIBLICAL EXAMPLES OF **JUST**

Joseph, the husband of Mary, was a **just** man (Matthew 1:19). When his promised wife was found to be with child, he realized his duty toward God in keeping the Jewish law. In the eyes of that law this woman was guilty of adultery, and she should be put away, or divorced. But Joseph must have felt affection for Mary because he wanted to put her away privately, lest she suffer the ridicule connected with a public example. Regardless of his emotions, however, Joseph's first thoughts were his duty toward God in keeping the law.

John the Baptist got into all sorts of trouble with Herod, but the Scriptures point out: "Herod feared John, knowing that he was a **just** man" (Mark 6:20). Certainly John realized the danger he faced in condemning the ruler's unlawful marriage to Herodias, but he was a **just** man. Duty to God in rebuking sin was more important to this disciple than literally saving his own neck.

Joseph of Arimathea is termed "a good man and just" (Luke 23:50). To befriend a condemned criminal was dangerous. Beneath a fear for his own safety, this counselor must have felt a sense of duty to God and to his fellowman. He **begged** for Christ's body and gave it a decent burial.

Cornelius was a **just** man—one that feared God (Acts 10:22). At the time the statement was made, this Gentile had not yet found the truth; but he was seeking. Note the ways in which he expressed his duty to God and to man: he gave alms to the people, prayed to God always and fasted (Acts 10:2, 30). When he heard the gospel, this sense of duty prompted him to do whatever God asked—even baptism (Acts 10:48).

Christ is the supreme example of the word **just**. In fact, Peter personified the term when he called Christ "the Just" (Acts 3:14). Pilate's wife called this Jewish prisoner a "just man" (Matthew 27:19). Christ realized His duty toward the Father. There had to be a sacrifice for sins as a propitiation, an appeasement. In performing this duty to Jehovah, our Lord performed a completely unselfish act toward man—the opportunity for salvation. "Christ also hath once suffered for sins, the just for the unjust, that he might bring us to God" (1 Peter 3:18).

JUST IN OUR LIVES

We admire these Bible characters for being **just. We** probably won't be called upon to put our lives in physical danger, but there are so many opportunities for us to cultivate this sense of duty to God and to our fellowman.

Worship—Does our sense of duty motivate us to assemble for worship (**every** opportunity for worship) even when we have a headache or a sniffle? True worship uplifts and is conducive to our spiritual well-being in and of itself. But we will have to admit that we are only human; there are occasions when worship means more to us than at other times. If we only worship when we **feel** like it, we may easily lose our appetite for spiritual food and die of starvation. A sense of duty is necessary for the establishment of proper habits. This realization of what is **just** or right will get us to the assembly during both the hills and valleys of our lives.

Money—Even though the money could be used to pay bills, does our sense of duty prompt us to put God first in our giving? I suppose every family has a legitimate place to put each dollar that is earned. There are **always** bills to be paid. Putting the Lord's part aside regularly over a period of years must be prompted by a sense of duty, a sense of what is just. Spontaneous giving has its place, but God demands a continuous giving of our means.

Duties toward our fellowman—People need other people. Sometimes we have to minister to their spiritual needs (teaching the Word of God); at other times we should do what we can to relieve their physical needs (caring for the necessities of the body); there are also very real emotional needs (companionship, just being there). We all feel more outgoing at times, but a sense of duty will help us respond to the problems of others even when we have our own worries.

Finally, brethren, whatsoever things pertain to your duty toward God and your fellowman . . . think on these things.

WORD STUDY OF **PURE**

We do not have too much trouble with this word **pure** (hagnos), for nearly everyone associates the same general meaning—chaste. The original word is used three other times in the Scriptures.

   (1) 1 Timothy 5:22: ". . . neither be partaker of other men's sins: keep thyself pure."

   (2) James 3:17: "But the wisdom that is from above is first pure, then peaceable. . ."

   (3) 1 John 3:3: "And every man that hath this hope (of seeing Christ) in him purifieth himself, even as he is pure."

PURE THOUGHTS IN THE TWENTIETH CENTURY

A Christian does not **plant** unchaste thoughts in his mind. True, they are all about us in this world. We cannot help being exposed to such ideas, but we do not dwell upon them. Just as quickly as they enter our minds, we should crowd them out of the way with good thoughts.

Many who would not dream of telling or listening to a smutty story or joke will nevertheless allow their minds to be filled with off-color thoughts through books and television. It doesn't matter what literary award a book has received. If it's filled with impure thoughts (I don't care how true to life they might be), a Christian doesn't need to be filling his subconscious mind with such ideas. Most movies are not fit to be seen. Not only innuendoes but blazen adultery and vile words characterize prime television viewing time. When these little seeds continually fall into our minds, they are **not** going to produce pure, chaste thoughts.

The thoughts that run through our minds should be so clean that they can always stand God's scrutiny.

Suggestions for Class Use

Lesson Five

1. Give a literal meaning of the original word for **just** (dikaios).
2. Discuss what Joseph (husband of Mary) did when he found his espoused wife with child before their marriage. How was Joseph a **just** man?
3. How did John the Baptist display his sense of justness in condemning Herod's marriage? What later happened to this cousin of Jesus?
4. Joseph of Arimathea was also a **just** man. How did he show his duty toward God and toward Christ?
5. In what ways was Cornelius a **just** man?
6. How did Christ view His suffering on the cross? What prompted the human side of His nature to go through the ordeal?
7. Appoint a panel to discuss **just** as it applies to our attitudes

toward worship, money and our duty toward our fellowman.

8. Express the meaning of **just** in our everyday lives.

9. What is the general meaning of **pure**?

10. **Pure** is used three other times in the New Testament. Read these aloud in class.

11. If we cannot **prevent** impure thoughts from entering our minds, what **can** we do about the situation?

12. Discuss the degradation of television programs during the prime viewing times. (As an outside assignment, ask each class member to watch carefully the programs that appear from seven o'clock until nine o'clock one evening, listing all the objectionable language. What effect is this bound to have upon a child's mind?)

13. Teacher, if you would like to try a little experiment to prove how much a picture or a suggestion can affect the subconscious, you might like to tape three different sheets of colored construction paper at the front of the room. Take them down, without comment, sometime during the middle of the class. At the end of the class period, see how many people can remember the colors. Even though these sheets of paper were just a part of the surroundings, they did make a stamp upon the subconscious.

LESSON SIX

WHATSOEVER THINGS ARE LOVELY AND OF GOOD REPORT

The word translated **lovely** is **prosphiles** and is used only in this Philippian passage. Its meaning is that which calls forth love, attractive, winsome, lovable, pleasing. Perhaps we can get a better **feel** of the word by considering some of its antonyms: vengeance, fear, bitterness, criticism. Some synonyms would be kindness, sympathy, forbearance, love.

PRACTICAL APPLICATIONS OF **LOVELY**

Have you ever been around those whose forked tongues knew only bitterness and criticism? Before they opened their mouths, you knew exactly the nature of the comments. I don't know about you, but I get an uncomfortable feeling around such people. In fact, I usually try to avoid them. There is enough of the bad in this world without incessantly harping upon it. A steady diet of looking for evil soon putrefies our minds. We will have to consciously replace bad thoughts with ones that are lovely if we don't want the same ugly feelings to crawl back. (Review the lesson concerning the unclean spirit in Matthew 12:43-45.)

The things that would be lovely to one person may have no appeal to another. **Every** person, however, has some thoughts that lift him to a higher plane. It is these wholesome, elevating thoughts that we should plant and cultivate in our subconscious minds. Long ago Alfred, Lord Tennyson expressed this same idea when he wrote:

Beauty seen is never lost,
God's colors all are fast;
The glory of this sunset heaven
Into my soul has passed.

One who had no physical eyesight penned these words:

What we have once enjoyed we can never lose.
A sunset, a mountain bathed in moonlight,
the ocean in calm and in storm—we see these,
love their beauty, hold the vision in our hearts.
All that we love deeply becomes a part of us.

                                        Helen Keller

The well-known author of the above words also said: "Use your eyes as if tomorrow you would be stricken blind." She further elaborated upon the sights she would wish to see if she had her eyesight restored for only three days: the faces of people whose kindnesses had made her life worth living, the face of a baby, books that had been read to her, the eyes of her faithful dogs, the freshness of nature in the woods, a dawn, places of culture, the faces of people on a busy street corner to understand daily lives and finally the faces of the suffering to know compassion. How many of these things we see daily and yet take for granted.

Perhaps many of you readers recall the plot of Thornton Wilder's play **Our Town,** in which the heroine is permitted to return from the dead to relive a day of her previous life. Simple joys which had formerly seemed so commonplace assumed a far greater meaning when viewed with a different perspective.

During elementary school days I learned a poem that made an impression on me. In "Barter" Sara Teasdale expressed these same ideas.

Life has loveliness to sell,
    All beautiful and splendid things,
Blue waves whitened on a cliff,

Soaring fire that sways and sings,
And children's faces looking up
Holding wonder like a cup.

Life has loveliness to sell,
   Music like a curve of gold,
Scent of pine trees in the rain,
   Eyes that love you, arms that hold,
And for your spirit's still delight,
Holy thoughts that star the night.

Spend all you have for loveliness,
   Buy it and never count the cost;
For one white singing hour of peace
   Count many a year of strife well lost,
And for a breath of ecstasy
Give all you have been, or could be.

An unknown writer expressed this thought: "What are you saving in your memory bin as food for the restless soul when the winter of life comes?" Old age is not the only winter of life. Hardships may come in earlier years. Memories can either be the strength we need to carry us through troubles or they may be unbearable burdens of regrets. At the close of each day think over the day's activities. Have we laid aside any precious events in our memory bins that will comfort us in years to come? Everyone needs a happiness collection—remembrances of simple, satisfying joys to pull out of the realm of the subconscious in trying times. To live in the past is unwise, but sometimes I fear that too many people have cut the ties with yesterday and are aimlessly drifting without plan or purpose. Memories can be a sturdy bridge under our feet as we cross from today into the uncertainties of tomorrow.

An unknown author said: "The best and most beautiful things in the world cannot be seen nor touched but are felt in the heart." "Though we travel the world over to find the beautiful, we must carry it with us or we will find it not " (Ralph Waldo Emerson).

WORD STUDY OF **GOOD REPORT**

It seems that the term "of good report" is only used in this passage in Philippians, so we have no basis of comparison with other Scriptures. The original word means: of good omen, auspicious, commendable, laudable. Hence, it implies favorable expression, praise, commendation.

APPLICATION OF **GOOD REPORT**

For weeks I had these definitions taped above my kitchen sink and mentally carried them around with me as I went about my routine household activities. I don't know that my thoughts are scholastically correct, but we'll talk them over anyway.

Circumstances of life are basically no different today than they were in Paul's time. Then, as now, the world was filled with the good and the bad. In reality, there were far more adverse external hardships with all the injustices of the day and lack of individual rights. Just how would one go about thinking of things of **good report** as he was being fed to the lions!

If we will only look hard enough, we can find blessings in all of life's circumstances. Everything that happens has its good. Often our tears of self-pity blind our eyes so that we cannot realize that the rocks in our paths can be steppingstones to a better life if we will only climb on top of them, straighten our backbones, and walk with courage. Nothing is all black or all white in this life. If we sincerely try to look for the things that are good, favorable and praiseworthy, we will usually find them.

The passage in Romans 8:28 used to bother me when I would see sincere Christians having such hard times as adverse circumstances took their toll. It has only been recently, after many years of literally wrestling with this passage, that I have begun to really understand what it means. GOD NEVER PROMISED TO CHANGE ANY EXTERNAL CIRCUM-STANCES IN OUR LIVES. INSTEAD, HE PROMISED TO CHANGE OUR FEELINGS TOWARD LIFE'S VICISSITUDES SO WE COULD FIND THE GOOD IN EVERYTHING. "Now no chastening for the present seemeth to be joyous, but grievous: nevertheless afterward it yieldeth the peaceable fruit of righteousness unto them which are exercised thereby" (Hebrews 12:11).

Finding the good in life depends upon the individual's point of view. Look at Napoleon. His life was the epitome of luxury and wealth. In spite of all his material possessions, toward the end of his days this ruler remarked: "I have never known six happy days in my life." In contrast, Helen Keller, the blind and deaf heroine of our day, commented: "I have found life so beautiful." One seemingly had all external circumstances necessary for a full life; the other had unbelievable handicaps. The latter looked for the good and found it. The former never bothered.

Montaigne, the French philosopher, expressed the same thought when he said: "A man is not hurt so much by what happens, as by his opinion of what happens." Far too many of us go through the **experiences** of suffering without ever learning the **lessons.**

Naturally, bad things will happen to us. Some we will bring upon ourselves, but many will be entirely beyond our control. If we will only stop to probe a little and really look for the good, we will find it. Happiness does not result from the pleasures of this life. Rather, it is a byproduct of victory over adversity. Instead of always looking at the black side of everything, try searching for the **good report,** the favorable view. God **promises** that **ALL** things will eventually work together for good for His children. Experiences that cause us to draw closer to God cannot be counted as adversity.

Let's look for the good report, the good side of people and situations. It's there. "If there be any virtue, if there be any praise, think on these things."

Suggestions for Class Use

Lesson Six

1. Discuss the meaning of **lovely** by considering its synonyms and antonyms. Is **prosphiles** used in any other passage?
2. Distinguish between a realization of the evil around us

and the constant dwelling upon wrongs.

3. We often stress the importance of putting bad thoughts from our minds. If these evil ideas are not replaced by good ones, what is the result? (Review the story in Matthew 12:43-45.) Can the mind remain as a vacuum?

4. Divide the class into small discussion groups. Allow several minutes for an exchange of ideas on the **lovely** things of this life. Note the variations in individual meanings of the word.

5. Do you agree or disagree with Helen Keller's thoughts concerning the advantages of storing up lovely thoughts?

6. Think back over yesterday's activities. Make a short list. Were any of your activities such that would bring fond recollections during difficult days and give you the strength to withstand hardships?

7. What is your opinion of the quotation: "The best and most beautiful things in the world cannot be seen or touched but are felt in the heart"?

8. What is the meaning of the term **of good report?**

9. Using reference books, discuss the conditions of life in Paul's day, including the attitude of government toward the rights of individuals. If you had been in Paul's shoes, could you have seen the favorable side of all his hardships? What is your opinion of this apostle's **thorn in the flesh** (2 Corinthians 12:7)?

10. How would you explain Romans 8:28 to a Christian who had just suffered some hardship in this life, such as the loss of a loved one, serious illness or financial adversity?

11. Allow each class member a few minutes to think over an apparent adversity in his life which later proved to be a blessing in disguise. Pool the thoughts of the class.

12. Why do you think Napoleon and Helen Keller had such different outlooks on life?

13. How may we go through the experiences of suffering without ever learning the lessons?

14. How may we bring adverse circumstances upon ourselves? Distinguish between these and circumstances beyond our control.

15. How can happiness be a product of victory over adversity?

16. Discuss the benefits of misfortunes that cause us to draw closer to God.

THE FRUIT OF THE SPIRIT IS LOVE

A Christian **must** produce fruit to be pleasing to God. Christ cursed the barren fig tree (Matthew 21:19) and condemned the man with one talent for failure to increase what God had given him (Matthew 25:14-30). When the **right** seeds are faithfully planted, the desired results **will** come. It is significant that the first fruit mentioned by Paul is **love,** perhaps the most poignant word in our language.

WORD STUDY OF **LOVE**

Love means many things to different people. The Greeks had four words which they used to express this idea. **Eros** was the word used for love between the sexes. It was a promiscuous love involving a passionate yearning after another person. **Philia** included sexual love but also involved the mind and the spirit. **Storge** meant family love. When Paul penned his epistle to the Galatians, however, he shunned these words and chose one foreign to secular Greek. **Agape** was a new word used to describe an attitude never attainable before Christianity.

God did not require a love that He had not first demonstrated. **Agape** is used in 1 John 4:8: "He that loveth not knoweth not God; for God **is** love." This **agape** love prompted God to give His only Son as a ransom for the sins of mankind: "For God so loved the world that he gave his only begotten Son, that whosoever believeth in him should not perish, but have everlasting life" (John 3:16). Because God loved us with **agape** love, we are to manifest this same kind of love toward **Him** and toward our **fellowmen.** This is a love that is a free act, definitely chosen by the subject. It is an overcoming of inborn emotions by the will of the mind. When we are insulted or humiliated, our natural emotions tell us to lash back with similar insults, but **agape** love causes the will to triumph over the animal instinct by substituting compassion for anger. No matter how deeply we may be hurt by someone, we will never seek anything but the best for the offender. The chief ingredient of this new love is self-sacrifice.

It is difficult to define anything as nebulous as love. Just as it is easier to see the outward manifestations of the wind than the wind itself, so is it better to define **agape** by giving tangible results of this new love. The Bible does not really try to **define** love. It **illustrates** this characteristic of a Christian. Paul lists the constituent elements in 1 Corinthians 13.

Love suffereth long. Love is patient. Love may sigh a bit, but it gladly stoops over and picks up the toys and clothes from the floor. **Love is kind.** Does kindness really need a definition? How tragic it is when people treat their pet dogs with more tenderness than they show their families. Love does not shout angry words and deliberately try to hurt the feelings of another. **We** may act that way, but that is not love. Love says, "Thank you for going to the trouble." It says, "I'm sorry." There are so many ways to say, "I love you." **Love envieth not.** Love trusts. It is neither jealous nor possessive. **Love vaunteth not itself, is not puffed up.** Love is humble. Love is not anxious to impress others with inflated ideas of its own importance. Some people cannot themselves feel important until they have made the ones around them seem **less** important. **Love doth not behave itself unseemly.** Love is courteous and polite; it has no place for rudeness. It does not pout, nor is it sullen. **Love seeketh not its own.** Love is unselfish in little and big things. It puts the welfare of others above personal desires. **Love is not easily provoked.** Love has an even temper. It is not touchy. **Love thinketh no evil.** Love expects and looks for the best, not the worst, in people. **Love rejoiceth not in iniquity but rejoiceth in the truth.** Love does not gloat over the shortcomings of others. It takes no delight in criticizing. **Love beareth all things.** Love knows no limit to its endurance. Most of us have only petty grievances. Others have real crosses to bear. **Love believeth all things.** Love knows no end to its trust. **Love hopeth all things.** Love expects the best of everything. We usually find what we're looking for. **Love endureth all things.** Love never fails. It survives all else.

MANIFESTATIONS OF LOVE

The love demanded by God is so devoted that all other commands are included in it. When the lawyer tempted Christ with the question: "Master, which is the great commandment in the law?" (Matthew 22:36), the inquirer was told to love God with all his being and secondly to love his neighbor as himself. The Lord went on to define a neighbor as any person in need of help.

God loves us with this **agape** love. He does not merely **say** that He loves us. Instead, He has proved, or manifested, His love by sending His Son into the world (1 John 4:9). When Peter claimed that he loved Christ, the Lord asked His apostle to prove it by feeding His lambs (John 21:15-17).

Soldiers wear uniforms as a manifestation of their occupation. Some religious people today, just as the Pharisees, use their dress as a display of their beliefs. True Christians have an outward sign to prove that they are truly disciples of Jesus: "A new commandment I give unto you, That ye love one another; as I have loved you, that ye also love one another. By this shall all men know that ye are my disciples, if ye have love one to another" (John 13:34, 35). Love is the undisputable litmus paper test of Christianity.

The Scriptures abound with reinforcements of this command. Time and again we are admonished to manifest this love by our actions toward all mankind.
   (1) "For all the law is fulfilled in one word, even in this; Thou shalt love thy neighbor as thyself" (Galatians 5:14).
   (2) "Seeing ye have purified your souls in obeying the truth

through the Spirit unto unfeigned love of the brethren, see that ye love one another with a pure heart fervently" (1 Peter 1:22).

(3) "We know that we have passed from death unto life, because we love the brethren. He that loveth not his brother abideth in death" (1 John 3:14).

(4) "And this is love, that we walk after his commandments" (2 John 6).

Agape love does not love just because someone is my brother and does nice things for me. **Anyone** could love under those circumstances. This new love has such depth and compassion that it prompts us to love even our enemies. "Ye have heard that it hath been said, Thou shalt love thy neighbor, and hate thine enemy. But I say unto you, Love your enemies, bless them that curse you, do good to them that hate you, and pray for them which despitefully use you, and persecute you" (Matthew 5:43, 44). This command was in opposition to Jewish tradition. It was a love that expected no return or repayment. It involved doing good to those who hate us. Peter was told to forgive a sinning brother seventy times seven (Matthew 18:21, 22). Such a compassionate heart was unknown to the Jewish traditions. In the Sermon on the Mount Christ even admonished the people to postpone their worship if a brother had some grievance against them until the matter could be settled (Matthew 5:23, 24).

The question as to who is the recipient of this love is secondary in importance. We do not love others for what **they** are but because of what **we** are, just as God loves us, not for our merits, but because of what **He** is. "We love him, because he first loved us" (1 John 4:19).

Love is mentioned in several other lists of Christian graces. "And now abideth faith, hope, charity, these three; but the greatest of these is charity" (1 Corinthians 13:13). "And above all these things put on charity, which is the bond of perfectness" (Colossians 3:14). "And beside this, giving all diligence, add to your faith . . . charity" (2 Peter 1:5-7).

Such an unselfish love would be impossible without the help of God. Humans could never manifest such a godly love by their own power. Only by planting the right seed can the fruit of **agape** love be produced. We can voice the thoughts of Paul when he said: "But by the grace of God I am what I am" (1 Corinthians 15:10).

Perhaps the cause of our failure to love other people as we should can be found in Romans 13:9: "Thou shall love thy neighbor as thyself." So much of our trouble in dealing with others stems from a dislike of self. A person who cannot accept himself certainly cannot accept his neighbor for what he is. Such people dislike others when they see the reflection of their own marred image. If we love ourselves properly (not an egotistical love), we **will** love our neighbors.

Suggestions for Class Use

Lesson Seven

1. Cite two instances to show that God expects fruit from the Christian.
2. Discuss the four words the Greeks used for **love.**
3. Why was **agape** love never really possible before Christianity?
4. How did God manifest His love toward mankind?
5. Contrast our natural reaction to insults with the reaction prompted by love.
6. What is the chief ingredient of this new love?
7. Compare the outward manifestations of love with the blowing of the wind.
8. Assign the characteristics of love mentioned in 1 Corinthians 13 to different class members for their interpretations.
9. How can the two commands mentioned in Matthew 22:36-40 be inclusive of all other commands?
10. How did Christ ask Peter to prove his love in John 21:15-17?
11. What is the Christian's outward sign of his love to Jesus (John 13:34, 35)?
12. Cite four Scriptures to reinforce the command mentioned in John 13:34, 35.
13. How was the new command given in Matthew 5:43, 44 in opposition to Jewish tradition?
14. If a brother has "ought against" us, what should we do before we worship (Matthew 5:23, 24)?

15. We love others not for what they are but because of what_____are. Discuss.
16. Discuss three other lists of Christian graces in which love is mentioned.
17. Could Christians manifest such an unselfish love without the help of God? How do we receive this help?
18. Let's get to the heart of love by applying **agape** love to these practical instances:
    (a) A brother tells some untruths about you. What would your reaction be?
    (b) You have been reprimanded by the elders for an activity which, in their judgment, is unwise. How should you receive the rebuke?
    (c) How should we treat a brother who is living in sin?
19. Ask each class member to give a personal example of an instance in which Christian love was, or should have been, applied.

THE FRUIT OF THE SPIRIT IS JOY

Abraham Lincoln certainly had the right idea when he said: "Most folks are about as happy as they make up their minds to be." I don't know about you, but I hate to see gloomy Christians! Some of my brethren act as if they had a steady diet of dill pickles and green persimmons for breakfast every morning. Christians, of all people, should radiate joy and happiness. Quite some time ago I read a little story in a church bulletin. It seems that a small child was quietly sitting by his mother's side during a service. He wasn't talking, squirming, tearing books or disturbing in any manner; he was just sitting there smiling. Finally his mother jerked him and in a whisper that could be heard for several rows rebuked him: "Stop that grinning! You're in church!"

The noun for joy, "chara," is used sixty times in the Scriptures and the verb form, meaning **rejoice,** is used 72 times. It is easier to run down references on the original use of a word than it is to put a finger on the real meaning. The joy to which Paul is referring is not a frivolous, giddy kind of gaiety. Practically every mature Christian can remember with nostalgia the enthusiastic joy of the young convert. He was going to take the world for Christ and no one could stop him. Usually one of two things happens. Either this stream of joy is dried up by the blazing sun (cares of the world) or else it deepens into an underground channel that is richer and fuller than the beginning one. Nehemiah 8:10 tells us that the joy of the Lord is our strength. What is this joy deep within the heart of a Christian?

THINGS THAT WILL NOT BRING JOY

Self-pity—Poor old Elijah was the epitome of self-pity as he sat under the juniper tree and requested death (1 Kings 19:4). Granted, he had a right to feel discouraged with Jezebel breathing down his neck with threats of death; but we can never find joy in constantly focusing our thoughts upon ourselves.

Fame—When the 70 returned with the ebullience of their ability to cast out devils, Christ admonished His disciples not to rejoice in this special gift which apparently brought fame to them but to rejoice because their names were written in heaven (Luke 10:20).

Material Possessions—Let's be honest with ourselves. Don't we spend most of our waking hours in acquiring or taking care of something to put **in** our stomachs, **on** our backs or **over** our heads? Yet Paul reminds us that "the kingdom of God is not meat and drink; but righteousness, and peace, and joy in the Holy Ghost" (Romans 14:17).

ADVICE FROM INSPIRED WRITERS

Since a Christian's joy is not the frivolous lightheartedness of this world, the child of God needs a new set of values. Let's turn to the inspired writers for their advice.

Christ—When we approach the throne of God with all our griefs and sorrows, our Mediator can say, "Father, I know just how they feel. I, too, have gone through many trials and tribulations." Isaiah prophesied of our Lord's rejection when he wrote: "He is despised and rejected of men; a man of sorrows, and acquainted with grief" (Isaiah 53:3). More than once the tears coursed down His face. The sins of His people precipitated His weeping over Jerusalem (Luke 19:41). On another occasion Christ wept at the tomb of His dear friend, Lazarus (John 11:35). In spite of all the sorrows in the life of our Supreme Example, Jesus very definitely experienced joy **at the same time** He was undergoing hardships more difficult than any of us will ever have to face. Could we feel joy if we were crucified? Christ did. "Who for the joy that was set before him endured the cross, despising the shame, and is set down at the right hand of the throne of God" (Hebrews 12:2). Only shortly before His death the Son of God spoke of joy: "These things have I spoken unto you, that my joy might remain in you, and that your joy might be full" (John 15:11). The same thought is expressed in the chapter immediately preceding His betrayal and arrest: "and these things I speak in the world, that they might have my joy fulfilled in themselves" (John 17:13).

John and Peter—John voiced the same teachings of the Master when he wrote: "And these things write we unto you, that your joy may be full" (1 John 1:4). Peter could see the joy in tribulations when he penned: "Wherein ye greatly rejoice, though now for a season, if need be, ye are in heaviness through manifold temptations" (1 Peter 1:6). In verse eight of the same chapter, the writer goes on to comment: "Ye rejoice with joy unspeakable and full of glory."

Paul—When you read through the pages of the New Testament, it seems that no one had more troubles than Paul. His stoning at Lystra gave great emphasis to his teaching that "we must through much tribulation enter into the kingdom of God" (Acts 14:22). He enumerated his hardships to the Corinthians in the sixth chapter of his second epistle to these Christians—afflictions, distresses, stripes, imprisonments and tumults (verses 4 and 5). When I viewed the dank, dark prison in which Paul was probably confined in Rome, I will have to admit that I wondered whether my faith would have been as strong under such adverse circumstances.

This devoted apostle told the Ephesian elders that he served the Lord with many tears (Acts 20:19). To the Romans he confessed that he had great heaviness and continual sorrow in his heart (Romans 9:2). Not all of Paul's troubles were physical in nature. Many were in the form of emotional grief caused by the wrongs of others. Party divisions, incest, marriage problems, eating meat offered to idols, the corruption of the Lord's Supper and many other sins plagued the band of followers which met at Corinth. Paul postponed a trip to this city so the wrongdoers could rectify their mistakes. He admonished them with written words: "For out of much affliction and anguish of heart I wrote unto you with many tears; not that ye should be grieved, but that ye might know the love which I have more abundantly unto you" (2 Corinthians 2:4).

In spite of all his physical and emotional trials, Paul could say that "none of these things move me" (Acts 20:24). He could even urge the Philippians: "Rejoice in the Lord alway: and again I say, Rejoice" (Philippians 4:4). The Thessalonians were told, "Rejoice evermore" (1 Thessalonians 5:16). Does this sound like a man who was wringing his hands and moaning, "Woe is me. Why has life dealt me so many blows when I've tried hard to do right?"

HOW CAN SORROW PRODUCE JOY?

Paul describes himself as sorrowful, yet always rejoicing (2 Corinthians 6:10). This enigma can only be solved when our faith is based upon the proper foundation. Paul throws further light on the subject when he said in Romans 15:13: "Now the God of hope fill you with all joy and peace in believing."

Such joy cannot be possible without an awareness that something is better than material possessions and the physical body. A Christian may undergo great pain in his physical body, but he is aware that one day he will have a "house not made with hands" (2 Corinthians 5:1). "If so be that we suffer with him, that we may be also glorified together" (Romans 8:17).

John tells us that sorrow can be turned into joy in the same manner that a woman forgets all the pain connected with the birth of a child when she holds her infant in her arms (John 16:20, 21). The reward is worth all the effort involved. Such an attitude is impossible unless a Christian has his sight set upon the final goal. If you have ever flown in bad weather, you will recall that it took only a few minutes for the airplane to rise above the rain-drenched clouds to the beauty of the sunlight above the storm. Far too many of us usually walk around with our noses glued to the ground instead of lifting our heads above the clouds.

The beatitudes describe the bliss and happiness of following Christ. Some translations render the word **blessed** as **happy,** but this can be deceptive. The English word **happy** contains the root word **hap** which means **chance.** Happiness is dependent upon chance and the circumstances of this life. The Greek word for **blessed** (makarios) has a different connotation. It implies a joy that is self-centered. It is untouchable by any misfortunes of life. This is a joy that sees us through any hardships which we may have to endure. Being joyful is better than being happy.

UPWARD, OUTWARD, INWARD

We may run the references of a word, study its various meanings and yet miss the whole idea. I believe the joy of which Paul is speaking in Galatians can best be defined by everyday illustrations. A Christian finds this joy as he looks upward, outward and inward.

Upward—A child of God has the joy of purpose in this life. Unlike the aimlessness and dissatisfaction of so many today who wander barefoot and unkempt, the child of God **knows** what he is here for. All else is subservient to that goal. "Let us hear the conclusion of the whole matter: Fear God, and keep his commandments: for this is the whole duty of man" (Ecclesiastes 12:13).

When we look upward, we could never find joy without the grace of God. Our very best service is not worthy of salvation. A realization of our inadequacies brings sorrow, not joy. But the grace of God throws a different light on the subject. We do all that we are commanded to the best of our ability to prove our willingness and then God's grace finishes what we are unable to do. Both joy (chara) and grace (charis) come from the same Greek root word. It is only when we realize our complete depravity that we can feel the real joy in salvation. David spoke of this joy when he said: "Restore unto me the joy of thy salvation" (Psalm 51:12) and "in thy presence is fulness of joy" (Psalm 16:11). It has been said that those who feel worse about their sins feel happiest about their forgiveness. Perhaps the reason we do not have as much joy in religion can be attributed to a lack of **hard** preaching today.

Outward—A Christian's joy is altruistic. It derives extreme satisfaction in thinking of others. I caught a glimpse of this joy not too long ago when two deacons witnessed the baptism of a man with whom they had been studying for three months. They literally beamed in this greatest of all joys. One Sunday night when I was seated behind a young mother, I saw joy etched on her face as she cuddled her baby and stroked his tiny head. I have seen young people discover how much more fun it is to make someone happy by a small, thoughtful act than it is to eat cookies and drink punch at a party. I heard a member reveal this same spirit of joy when she spoke of caring for an invalid relative for so many, many years. With tears in her eyes she said, "I've enjoyed every minute of it."

A Christian derives joy from fulfilling his duty, no matter how unpleasant it may seem. Think back over the years. Didn't you feel a real sense of accomplishment when you handed in a required paper in school? As much as you hated to do it, when the task was completed, you felt that you had done what you were supposed to do; and there was real satisfaction. It may seem crude, but I even feel a certain amount of joy when I wash my hands and stand back to view my freshly cleaned oven!

Inward—A Christian's joy comes from introspection. It results not only from lifting our eyes upward and outward but also inward. Think over the events which have brought you lasting joy. I have. Joy has nothing to do with **things.** After five weeks in the intensive care unit of a hospital following an automobile accident, how well I remember my first breakfast of solid food when the doctors removed the stomach tubes and unwired my jaws. I had never dreamed bacon and eggs could taste so wonderful! Weeks later I again shed tears of joy when I took my first steps and knew that my legs were one day going to walk once again.

"The selfsame well from which your laughter rises was oftentimes filled with your tears . . . The deeper that sorrow

carves into your being, the more joy you can contain . . .
When you are joyous, look deep into your heart and you
shall find it is only that which has given you sorrow is giving
you joy. When you are sorrowful look again within your
heart, and you shall see that in truth you are weeping for
that which has been your delight.''

Kahil Gibran

from **The Prophet**

Suggestions for Class Use

Lesson Eight

1. Contrast the initial joy which you felt as a new Christian
   with your feelings now. What usually happens to the
   enthusiasm of the new convert?
2. How can self-pity, fame and material possessions fail to
   bring joy? Add other false standards of joy.
3. Give three examples of sorrow in the life of Christ.
4. How could our Lord experience joy in the hardships of
   the cross? (Hebrews 12:2)
5. Consider two other passages depicting the joy of Christ
   (John 15:11; 17:13). How was such an attitude possible?
6. Who made these statements: "And these things write we
   unto you, that your joy may be full"; "Wherein ye greatly
   rejoice, though now for a season, if need be, ye are in
   heaviness through manifold temptations"?
7. Divide the class into four discussion groups to consider the
   hardships and sorrows of Paul as found in 2 Corinthians
   6:4, 5; Acts 20:19; Romans 9:2; 2 Corinthians 2:4. Compile
   the findings.
8. Give three Scriptures to prove that Paul rejoiced in his
   afflictions.
9. We can rejoice in afflictions only when our faith is based
   upon what?
10. What should be the Christian's attitude toward his
    physical body?
11. What do you think of John's comparison of joy and
    sorrow with the experiences of birth?
12. How can the term **happy** be deceptive in the beatitudes?
    Is true joy ever based upon chance?
13. How can a purpose in life give joy? What is the whole

duty of man?
14. What part does God's grace play in a Christian's joy?
15. Ask each class member to list two instances in which he received great joy from thinking of others. Share these experiences.
16. Have you ever felt joy from doing an unpleasant task that had to be done? Why?
17. Think back over some of the sorrows of your life. In reality, weren't you weeping for something which had previously brought you joy? Would you be willing to forego the joy in order never to experience the sorrow?
18. In your own words, summarize the meaning of the joy of the Christian.
19. Discuss Addison's comment in class: "What sunshine is to flowers, smiles are to humanity. They are but trifles to be sure; but scattered along life's pathway, the good they do is inconceivable."

LESSON NINE

THE FRUIT OF THE SPIRIT IS PEACE

Peace has become the **in** word for today. Peace signs and symbols are all about us, but very few people seem to possess any degree of real peace. Buildings and cars have been burned, protests have been staged and innocent people have even been killed—all in the name of peace. Somehow I have never been able to understand the message such advocates have been trying to get across. Neither are apathy and carelessness to be confused with peace. Wearing dirty clothes and seldom taking baths also seem to be poor methods of promoting peace. Countless numbers seek peace in LSD trips. Others withdraw by means of alcohol. Drunks literally lying in the gutters of large cities attest to th futility of such escape measures. Many are in mental hospitals because they seek peace by escaping reality.

In our Bible classes we study a great deal about peace. We sing about it: "Peace Be Still." I am certain most of you know the hymn: "Dear Lord and Father of Mankind." I get a stab of conscience whenever I sing that last stanza: "And may our **ordered** lives confess the beauty of thy peace." I always think about my kitchen cabinets and hall closets. Somehow my life doesn't seem very **ordered.**

WORD STUDY OF **PEACE**

The Greek word used by Paul is eirene. Its meanings include **unity, concord, calmness** and **tranquility** of mind and heart. The word corresponds to the Hebrew word **shalom**, which implies not just freedom from trouble but everything that makes for man's best good.

USES IN THE SCRIPTURES

God's Word abounds with admonitions to live peaceably. 1 Corinthians 14:33 stresses that God is not the author of confusion but of peace. Jehovah is referred to as the God of peace in Romans 16:20 and Hebrews 13:20. The promised child is called the Prince of Peace in Isaiah 9:6. In the Sermon on the Mount Christ pronounced His blessings on the peacemakers (Matthew 5:9). Paul admonished the Christians at Rome: "If it be **possible,** as much as lieth in you, live peaceably with all men" (Romans 12:18). Evidently Paul must have realized that there would be difficulties in living up to this admonition!

God's wisdom is characterized by this trait. "But the wisdom that is from above is first pure, then peaceable" (James 3:17). Peace makes itself evident in unity (Ephesians 4:3). It is only through the strength of God that one can have peace with death (Psalm 23:4).

ENIGMA

For centuries mankind has searched for peace—peace with himself, his neighbor and his God. Its achievement seems hopelessly impossible at times, but we do have a promise that such a peace is attainable. "And the peace of God, which passeth all understanding, shall keep your hearts and minds through Christ Jesus" (Philippians 4:7). (Note that this verse immediately precedes the verse containing the seeds used in our study.)

PEACE IMPOSSIBLE FOR THE WICKED

There can be no peace for those who do not follow God's ways. "There is no peace, saith the Lord, unto the wicked" (Isaiah 48:22). Jeremiah prophesied of the hopelessness of

Jerusalem and Judah when they would say, "Peace, peace; when there is no peace" (Jeremiah 6:14). It was to the righteous, not the wicked, that peace was promised: "And the work of righteousness shall be peace" (Isaiah 32:17).

HOW?

"And the fruit of righteousness is sown in peace of them that make peace" (James 3:18). There are some things that **make** for peace (Romans 14:19). Having the Word of God in our hearts would be placed near the top of the list. We use Colossians 3:16 so often in proving that we must worship God without the aid of instrumental music, but how often do we fail to notice the first part of that passage and also the verse immediately preceding: **"And let the peace of God rule in your hearts,** to the which also ye are called in one body; and be ye thankful. **Let the word of Christ dwell in you richly in all wisdom . . ."** There seems to be some connection between peace and having the Word of Christ in us. Hundreds of years before, David also observed this great truth: "Great peace have they which love thy law" (Psalm 119:165). Isaiah essentially said the same thing: "Thou wilt keep him in perfect peace, whose mind is stayed on thee" (Isaiah 26:3). Justification by our faith also promotes peace: "Therefore being justified by faith, we have peace with God through our Lord Jesus Christ" (Romans 5:1).

PEACE CONTRASTED WITH CONFLICT

To think that peace is the absence of conflict is to miss the whole idea. The same One who said: "Blessed are the peacemakers" (Matthew 5:9) also said: "Think not that I am come to send peace on earth: I came not to send peace, but a sword" (Matthew 10:34). Perhaps the meaning can best be understood by using a very common illustation. We have had a sense of false peace among nations for a number of years. More technically, the situation has been called a **cold war.** Although open conflict has not erupted among certain nations, many feelings of discontent are prevalent. Real peace comes—not by a mere cessation of arms—but by the conquest of one side over another. It is by the same comparison that Christians find peace. They have conquered. They are the victors. The child of God can withstand all sorts of physical ordeals because "... in all these things we are more than conquerors through him that loved us" (Romans 8:37).

(1) **Christians are the victors over evil.** God's children know the allures of Satan. They have wrestled with temptations; but, with the help of God, they have emerged victorious. Each time they say **no** to wrong, they experience a little more of this peace. As painful as the process may be, young people become victorious when they encounter temptation and learn to say **no**. "For whatsoever is born of God overcometh the world: and this is the **victory** that overcometh the world, even our faith" (1 John 5:4).

(2) **Christians are victorious over the vicissitudes of this life.** "Each one has to find his peace from within, and peace to be real must be unaffected by outside circumstances" (Mahatmah Gandhi). Christians meet many discouraging circumstances, many of which seem totally unfair. They encounter many thorns along the way. Their lives are filled with peace, not because their paths have been strewn with roses, but because they have risen above adversities. Instead of cursing fate, they have accepted their lots in life and have made the most of the situation. I have seen this peace in the eyes of the people who have faced overwhelming physical infirmities. True, there had been a conflict; but the victory of spirit over body brought the ensuing peace. Legs may not work, hands may no longer grasp; yet some are able to come out victorious in this struggle. Many others succumb and wallow in self-pity.

(3) **Christians are victorious over self.** "Nothing can bring you peace but yourself" (Ralph Waldo Emerson). Peace with self is not a gift but rather a difficultly earned achievement, a result of victory. Christians know what they want out of life. All else falls into its proper place. Because their eyes are set on their goals, the daily clutter of life does not become paramount. In maturity they have learned that they could **never** do enough to **earn** salvation. They **will** not be perfect. They **cannot** be perfect. But they have an intercessor who knows the frustrations of living in a human body. They know they are on the right path and also realize there is an

understanding hand to guide and help when they stumble. Only then can they experience the peace that passeth understanding.

Suggestions for Class Use

Lesson Nine

1. Why do you suppose the search for so-called **peace** has become so prominent today?
2. Contrast the seeming objectives of peace advocates with their methods of achieving their goals. For what do you think they are really searching?
3. What is the meaning of the Greek word for peace (eirene)?
4. Discuss these Scriptures in reference to God's desire for peace: 1 Corinthians 14:33; Romans 16:20; Hebrews 13:20; Matthew 5:9.
5. Why do you suppose the phrase **if it be possible** was included in Romans 12:18?
6. How can we have peace with death?
7. Divide into smaller groups to discuss "the peace of God, which passeth all understanding." Why are we promised a peace which we cannot understand?
8. Consider these verses: Isaiah 48:22; Jeremiah 6:14; Isaiah 32:17. Why is real peace impossible for the wicked? Paradoxically, why do the wicked often seem to have the easiest lot in life?
9. How can having God's Word in our hearts foster peace in our lives? How can we get His Word into our minds?
10. How can you justify these two passages in Matthew (5:9; 10:34)?
11. In a brainstorming session, on the board list some examples of smoldering conflicts between nations during the **cold war.** Compare this situation to similar conflicts between individuals.
12. Do you agree that a real victory is needed for true peace?
13. On a slip of paper have each class member list one remembrance of a personal victory over evil. Call for volunteers to share their victories in a class discussion.
14. Both from personal experiences and public knowledge, cite some examples of people who have been victorious over

the seemingly unjust circumstances of life.

15. Why is victory over self (inner conflicts) perhaps the most difficult victory of all?

16. Do you agree with this definition of anxiety: "preoccupation with things of lesser importance in the belief that if they are cared for, all will run smoothly"?

17. Paul urged Timothy to pray for whom to promote peace (1 Timothy 2:1, 2)?

18. Should we desire peace at any price?

19. How can you have peace with someone who doesn't want it?

20. Paul urged Christians to "be at peace among yourselves" (1 Thessalonians 5:13). How can there be peace in the church when there are differences of opinion? See Romans 14:1-10.

LESSON TEN

THE FRUIT OF THE SPIRIT IS LONGSUFFERING

Franklin rightfully observed: "He that can have patience can have what he will." Be honest. Haven't we all prayed for more patience (longsuffering) at one time or another? The only trouble is that our approach is all wrong. We're getting the cart before the horse when we make an outright request for patience.

WORD STUDY

The Greek word **makrothumia** may quite literally be translated **makros** (long) and **thumos** (temper). We all know what a short temper is. **Makrothumia** is the direct opposite. It means suffering long. Synonyms would be steadfastness, endurance, forbearance and patience.

Longsuffering does not imply just a shallow good nature. Some people may be too lazy to react or too proud to respond when attacked. Others may be more insensitive to criticism. Our **reason** for patience is just as important as the trait itself. There is also a difference between real patience and sullen endurance.

The connotations of the word are varied. To some, **longsuffering** means the ability to endure personal injuries or irritations without being provoked to anger. Christ is a supreme

76

example of this quality. To others it implies the ability to wait without becoming irritated. "They also serve who only stand and wait" (Milton). To still others the word means persistence in doing the menial tasks of life without complaining.

OTHER PASSAGES

Sometimes we can best get the **feel** of a word by examining it in other contexts. Paul uses this word in describing God: "Or despisest thou the riches of his goodness and forbearance and longsuffering; not knowing that the goodness of God leadeth thee to repentance?" (Romans 2:4). In the great **love** chapter we are told that love suffers long (1 Corinthians 13:4). We prove ourselves to be ministers of God by our longsuffering (2 Corinthians 6:6). Paul told the Colossians to "put on . . . long-suffering" (Colossians 3:12). "Behold, we count them happy which endure" (James 5:11). If we are to be worthy of our Christian vocation, we must possess longsuffering (Ephesians 4:1, 2).

BIBLICAL EXAMPLES

In the fifth chapter of his epistle James cites three examples of patience. In verse seven the writer admonishes Christians to wait for the coming of Christ with the same patience as a farmer waits for his crops to ripen. In the tenth verse reference is made to the afflictions and patience of the prophets, who suffered because they were doing right. "For what glory is it, if, when ye be buffeted for your faults, ye shall take it patiently? but if, when ye do well, and suffer for it, ye take it patiently, this is acceptable with God (1 Peter 2:20). "For it is better, if the will of God be so, that ye suffer for well doing, than for evil doing" (1 Peter 3:17). Hebrews 11:38 tells us that we are not worthy of these Old Testament martyrs. James concludes his illustrations of patience by referring to Job, the epitome of endurance.

Consider the great patience of David in dealing with Saul as the king tried to take the life of the former shepherd. David's procrastination in assuming the throne was not due to laziness or inactivity. He simply realized that it was not time.

Contrast the lack of patience which Peter displayed when he cut off the ear of the servant of the high priest (John 18:10) with the endurance he possessed in the fourth chapter of Acts.

Paul certainly was not very longsuffering when we first encounter his story in the Scriptures as he persecuted the early Christians, but he changed so radically that he was even willing to become all things to all men if it aided in winning souls (1 Corinthians 9:19-23). He admonished the young preacher Timothy to preach the word with all longsuffering (2 Timothy 4:2).

Christ spoke a parable concerning the patience needed in the forgiving of our brother's faults when Peter asked Him how often it was necessary to forgive someone. "Then came Peter to him, and said, Lord, how oft shall my brother sin against me, and I forgive him? till seven times? Jesus saith unto him, I say not unto thee, Until seven times; but, Until seventy times seven" (Matthew 18:21, 22). (Note the parable in verses 23-35 of the same chapter.)

Jehovah Himself is a supreme example of patience. His longsuffering was evident while Noah was building the ark and preaching (1 Peter 3:20). When He spoke directly to Moses in the giving of the Ten Commandments, God proclaimed that He was "merciful and gracious, longsuffering, and abundant in goodness and truth" (Exodus 34:6). Dealing with His people through forty years of wilderness wanderings caused even the Father to become exasperated at times. (See Deuteronomy 9:19, 20; 13:17.) The New Testament extends the idea of God's patience with man. "The Lord is not slack concerning his promise, as some men count slackness; but is longsuffering to us-ward, not willing that any should perish, but that all should come to repentance" (2 Peter 3:9). As mentioned previously, God's goodness, forbearance and longsuffering are instrumental in leading men to repentance (Romans 2:4).

Patience is certainly not an insipid virtue. Instead of showing indifference or approval of sin, a patient person displays understanding.

HOW OBTAINED

We should not ask God for patience. Instead, we should fill our minds with the right things—thoughts that are true, honest, just, pure, lovely, of good report—cultivate the ground properly, and patience slowly germinates and produces perhaps the loveliest flower of all. We demand the fruit without all the cares of cultivation.

Patience involves acceptance of conditions over which we have no control. We may not understand now, but Christians have the assurance that all things will work together for good eventually (Romans 8:28). Someone has said that the secret of patience is doing something constructive in the meantime.

Patience can never be developed until we have cultivated a proper sense of values, which is a trait of maturity. There **are** things important enough to cause us to lose our patience. We're not expected to endure everything stoically. Our Lord was so exasperated with the money changers that He drove them out of the Temple (Matthew 21:12). But His exasperation was over important grievances. It has been said that we may be judged by the **nature** of the things which upset us. This has been called our **tension capacity.**

When **things** are uppermost in our sense of values, a broken dish **does** seem like a catastrophe. But, to a Christian, a **broken heart** is far more important. Which bothers us more— dirt found on the knees of pants and tracked on the floor, or smut that pollutes the mind? Is a messed up house more worthy of our concern than the messed up life of a friend? Are our egos so weak that we lose patience with anyone who damages the image which we hold of ourselves?

It has only been in recent times that I have really understood how "tribulation worketh patience" (Romans 5:3) or how the "trying of your faith worketh patience" (James 1:3). Logic and human reasoning would seem to tell us that vexations, great and small, cause us to lose our patience instead of improving it. Some people lose their faith and go to pieces when trouble comes. Others are drawn closer to God in their longsuffering of similar trials. The difference seems to be the cultivated soil. Our **attitude** about tribulations determines whether they are ladders to improvement or shovels of despair. When we depend upon ourselves, we lose patience because we can't cope with problems alone. When we admit our weakness and depend upon a greater source of strength, we become strong (2 Corinthians 12:10). We must develop an inner reserve or stability if we are to cope with the crushing pressures of the world. Tribulations also broaden our understanding. We may condemn a person's shortcomings. When we're faced with similar trials, however, we may discover that it isn't always easy to do the right thing. We become a little more understanding when we slip into the shoes of another and feel the same rocks in the pathway.

WEEDS

We may have the best of intentions and honestly try to plant the right seeds in our minds, but so many different weeds can choke the sprouting plants. Let's be honest with ourselves. When we hurry here and there, running behind our self-imposed timetable with last minute details, don't petty annoyances get under our skin much more than when we're relaxed and not pushing ourselves so much? You know the answer as well as I do. Each one of us could produce much healthier fruits of patience if we would do a little weeding in our lives. It's so hard to do, but it can produce amazing results.

CLOSING THOUGHTS

"Patience is power; with time and patience, the mulberry leaf becomes silk" (Chinese Proverb).

"How poor are they who have not patience! What wound did ever heal but by degrees" (Shakespeare).

"It's easy finding reasons why other folks should be patient."

"The journey of a thousand miles begins with a single step" (Lao-Tse).

Suggestions for Class Use

Lesson Ten

1. Discuss both the literal meaning of **makrothumia** and the everyday usage of **longsuffering.**

2. Contrast true patience with the trifling, "no good" attitude of some.

3. Give concrete examples of these connotations of long-suffering: (a) ability to endure personal injuries without being provoked to anger; (b) ability to wait without being irritated; (c) persistence in doing menial tasks.

4. How is the same original word used in these passages: Romans 2:4; 1 Corinthians 13:4; 2 Corinthians 6:6; Colossians 3:12; James 5:11; Ephesians 4:1, 2?

5. Assign a class member to discuss the three examples of patience mentioned in the fifth chapter of James.

6. Why did David not assume the throne when he was annointed?

7. How did Peter's patience develop?

8. Paraphrase the parable in Matthew 18:23-35 in modern language.

9. Trace Jehovah's patience in dealing with His people.

10. What is the difference in patience with the sins of others and indifference, or approval, of them?

11. Should we ever ask God for patience? Justify your answer.

12. Do you agree that the secret of patience is doing something constructive in the meantime? What are some constructive activities?

13. Why is a proper sense of values a prerequisite to patience? What things usually upset us most?

14. How can tribulation possibly work patience?

15. Cite some concrete examples of your change in attitude toward the problems of others when you were faced with the same trials.

16. Divide into smaller groups to discuss the weeds in our lives that choke patience. Be specific! What can we do about them?

17. Turn to the section entitled CLOSING THOUGHTS and allow a few minutes for silent reading and thought. Share your conclusions at the end of that time.

THE FRUIT OF THE SPIRIT IS GENTLENESS AND GOODNESS

The King James translation of the Greek word **chrestotes** is **gentleness,** but the same word is translated **kindness** in a number of passages (2 Corinthians 6:6, Ephesians 2:7; Colossians 3:12; Titus 3:4) and as **goodness** in others (Romans 2:4; Romans 11:22). Other synonyms would be uprightness and generosity. It is used by classical writers to denote goodness or excellence of character and suggests a gentle hand of love and a soft answer.

The next word in Galatians 5:22, which is translated **goodness,** is actually a different Greek word—**agathosune.** This is peculiarly a Bible word and does not occur in secular Greek. In fact, it is found only three other times in the New Testament (Romans 15:14; Ephesians 5:9 and 2 Thessalonians 1:11). It is rather difficult to distinguish between the two words, but it seems that **chrestotes** implies a kind disposition toward others whereas **agathosune** is a practical manifestation of kindness, or kindness at work. Since the two words are parallel in their meanings, we will consider them as one unit in this study.

PRACTICAL DEFINITION

All of us have known individuals who seem to possess this special trait of kindness. We love to be around them because they make us feel good inside. When you get right down to it, **kindness involves thoughtfulness above and beyond what is expected.** When we pay our electric bills, we are not showing kindness; we are doing what is expected. Neither is the power board showing kindness when it supplies electricity. So much of this life revolves around the **what's in it for me** philosophy. **I'll do for you what is expected and not one bit more.** Kindness says, "I know I don't have to do this and it really isn't expected, but I want to because I think a lot of you."

When the little children were brought to the Savior to be touched, He not only touched them; He took them up in His arms (Mark 10:13-16). We, too, should follow His example and do more than what is expected of us. There is no place for Christians who are **loners.** We must be willing to crawl out of our shells and lend a helping hand wherever it is needed. Pride produces unkindness, but humility fosters kindness.

BIBLICAL EXAMPLES

The well-loved story of the good Samaritan (Luke 10:25-37) is a classical example of kindness in action. The Samaritan, like the priest and Levite, did not **have** to help the man in distress; but this one had compassion (the key to the matter) and wanted to render whatever service would be helpful. Without this compassion, service to others assumes the mask of hypocrisy. It is this gentleness in our hearts **(chrestotes)** that prompts us to the action of goodness **(agathosune).**

WRONG USES OF KIND DEEDS

The Scriptures give numerous examples of kind actions with the wrong motive. Jacob did a noble thing when he gave red pottage to hungry Esau (Genesis 25:29-34), but the motive was a selfish one. Jael was generous to Sisera when she gave him a bottle of milk and covered him, but she later nailed him to the ground (Judges 4:17-22). Delilah spoke words of love to Samson (Judges 16:4-31), but her motive was wrong. She was scheming to discover the source of her lover's strength. Satan offered three wonderful gifts to Christ during the temptation (Matthew 4:1-11), but these gestures were hardly from a compassionate heart!

THE GOODNESS OF GOD

The goodness of God **(chrestotes)** is mentioned in Romans 2:4: ". . . the goodness of God leadeth thee to repentance." Throughout the centuries, Jehovah has shown His gentleness, or goodness, to unappreciative mankind. In spite of their disobedience, the Israelites were the recipients of God's favor and blessings for hundreds of years. Today Christians receive so many blessings from the hand of God. It is only by the kindness of God that we receive the gift of life, but we take it for granted. Although we make many mistakes and are ungrateful for all our blessings, He continues, day after day, to give us so many good things. Even when we try to do our best, we could never **earn** our salvation. It is only through the kindness of God that we receive eternal life in Him. "That in the ages to come he might shew the exceeding riches of his grace in his kindness toward us through Christ Jesus. For by grace are ye saved through faith; and that not of yourselves: it is the gift of God" (Ephesians 2:7, 8).

OUR KINDNESS TOWARD OTHERS

Kindness finds expression in so many ways. It **looks** for ways to do little things for others—unexpected thoughtfulness. I have mused over this word for several weeks as I have vacuumed, washed dishes and gone about routine activities. I've thought about all the acts of kindness—things which I didn't deserve—that others have shown me during my lifetime and have reached the conclusion that such deeds could fill a book. During a critical illness several years ago, kindness fed my family for weeks when I could not cook. It prompted others to sit with my loved ones day and night throughout weeks of long hours of waiting at the hospital so they wouldn't have to face bad news alone. Kindness was personified in the person who took my children shopping at this time so they could buy their little gifts for the holidays. Kindness bought my daughter white gloves for a Girl Scout program and went with her because all the other girls had mothers there to watch them proudly. Kindness came by the house to sew a badge on a Cub Scout uniform for my son because I couldn't hold a needle. Kindness prompted a teenage boy to buy three red roses and have a cake baked and iced with the words "Welcome Home" when I returned from the hospital. I could go on and on. So many of my brethren have shown me what kindness **really** means—far more eloquently than just knowing the definitions of the Greek word.

Often kindness can penetrate the hearts of others when all else has failed. One of Aesop's Fables tells the story of a contest between the wind and the sun to determine which of the two was more powerful. The wind blew and howled around the man in an effort to get him to remove his coat, but he only pulled it more tightly around him. It was the warmth of the sun which eventually caused the man to shed his coat.

Several years ago while I was doing door-to-door work in a mission effort, I ran across a woman who said that she was not interested in a correspondence course or the Bible filmstrips at that time but she would like for us to remember her daughter, who was very ill in the hospital. We put her name on our card list in our zone work when we returned home and a number of people sent cards to this woman. Several weeks later I received a most appreciative note from the daughter in which she said: "I want to meet some of your people. I asked my mother about that church and why so many would take time to write someone they don't know. She told me that your people were a loving and caring kind. I truly believe this and want to say thanks again. There should be more of this kind of love in our world."

Most of us have good impulses, but we procrastinate and fail to put them into action. This week, starting right now, why not resolve **each day** to **seek** some unexpected way of showing kindness to at least one person. At the end of a year, three hundred and sixty-five people will be a little happier because you cared enough to do something.

Suggestions for Class Use

Lesson Eleven

1. The word **chrestotes** is translated by what three words in the King James' translation? After considering its use in the passages listed in the lesson, what is its definition in

your words?

2. How would you distinguish between the meanings of **chrestotes** (gentleness) and **agathosune** (goodness)?

3. Do you agree or disagree with the statement: "Kindness involves thoughtfulness above and beyond what is expected"?

4. Can a Christian live a life apart from the trials and concerns of others?

5. What was the key to the response of the good Samaritan?

6. Jacob, Jael, Delilah and Satan all did compassionate things for someone. What was wrong with their actions?

7. How can both the goodness of God (Romans 2:4) and His chastisement lead us to repentance?

8. Let each class member take time to make an individual list of the blessings which God has bestowed. Share these lists with the class. Could we in any way deserve all that God has done for us?

9. Divide into smaller groups to discuss ways in which other people have been thoughtful toward us. Compile these findings in a general class discussion. (Teachers, don't overlook the value of discussion in smaller groups. Many shy people will express themselves under these circumstances whereas they freeze in a classroom discussion.)

10. In Aesop's Fable about the wind and the sun, which element was more effective? Why?

11. Ask each class member to make a list of several unexpected kindnesses which he hopes to show to others during the next week. Don't discuss since this is a private matter, but ask each one to remember his commitment in his own personal prayers.

12. Is there any limit to the kindness which I should show others? What about unreasonable demands on my time?

LESSON TWELVE

THE FRUIT OF THE SPIRIT IS FAITH

The original word for faith is **pistis**, which carries with it the idea of faithfulness, reliability, loyalty, confidence. It is a firm persuasion, a conviction, based upon hearing. The American Standard Version translates the word as **faithfulness,** a quality which flows from faith in God. **Pistis** is used commonly in secular Greek for trustworthiness.

USES IN THE SCRIPTURES

Pistis is used to denote **trust** in the following passages:

1 Corinthians 2:5—"That your faith should not stand in the wisdom of men, but in the power of God."

1 Corinthians 15:14—"If Christ be not risen, then is our preaching vain, and your faith is also vain."

Galatians 3:24—"Wherefore the law was our schoolmaster to bring us unto Christ, that we might be justified by faith."

1 Thessalonians 3:2—"And send Timotheus, our brother, and minister of God, and our fellowlabourer in the gospel of Christ, to establish you, and to comfort you concerning your faith."

It is this trust or confidence in God which enables the Christian to say: "And we know that all things work together for good to them that love God" (Romans 8:28). Absolutely nothing (except ourselves) can separate us from the love of God (Romans 8:38, 39).

Pistis is also used to denote **trustworthiness** in Matthew 23:23: "Woe unto you, scribes and Pharisees, hypocrites! for ye pay tithe of mint and anise and cummin, and have omitted the weightier matters of the law, judgment, mercy, and faith: these ought ye to have done, and not to leave the other undone." The word also carries with it the same meaning in Romans 3:3: "For what if some did not believe? shall their unbelief make the faith of God without effect?" In Acts 17:31 the word is translated **assurance.** In Matthew 8:10 the faith mentioned is one of great or unusual belief: "I have not found so great faith, no, not in Israel." **Reliability** is implied in 1 Corinthians 16:13: "Watch ye, stand fast in the faith." It is this faith which makes possible faithfulness unto death (Revelation 2:10).

GOD'S FAITHFULNESS

Psalm 91 is a most beautiful account of the faithfulness and reliability of the Lord. Read it to gain insight into the loyalty of God toward His people. His faithfulness is not occasional nor peripheral. Neither is it subject to the whims of man. When God says He will do something, He **will** do it. Nor is His faithfulness to be contradicted by His waiting. When we meet His conditions, Jehovah's promises will come true. The reward may not be imminent. There may be a lifetime of waiting, but God will do what He says. Consider the promises made to Abraham in Genesis 12:1, 2; 15:5; and 17:1-8. It was years after the death of Abraham before the land and great nation promises were fulfilled. Hundreds of years passed before all nations of the earth were blessed through the coming of the Messiah, but God was reliable. He did what He said He would do. Noah had to wait for one hundred and twenty years to see the fulfillment of divine promises, but Noah did his part. When the time came, God did **His** part. Faith in the reliability of God should remove anxiety from our lives.

OBEDIENCE NECESSARY

Our faith depends upon our obedience and attitude toward God. With David we can say, "I have chosen the way of truth: thy judgments have I laid before me" (Psalm 119:30).

Many of the Hebrews could not enter into the promised land because of their unbelief (Hebrews 3:19). God had promised the land to them, but they did not believe they were strong enough to take the area away from their enemies when the spies brought back their reports to the people (Numbers 13:17 - 14:39). Unbelief usually leads to disobedience.

NOT BASED UPON OUTWARD MANIFESTATIONS

Faithfulness or loyalty to God is not based solely upon an outward show. The Israelites offered polluted bread (probably molded) on the altar and sickly animals for sacrifices (Malachi 1:7, 13-14). Their actions of disrespect and defiance were caused by their attitude: "Behold, what a weariness it is!" (Malachi 1:13). Today we don't offer moldy bread or a lame animal for worship, but how many times do we **go through the motions** of worship while offering God only the leftovers of our lives?

PRACTICAL APPLICATIONS

Our loyalty and reliability should continue after the initial spurt of enthusiasm which is characteristic of new Christians has waned. The parable of the soils warns that many will gladly receive the word but will quickly wither when the sun's rays strike because they have no roots (Matthew 13:5, 6). If a young Christian can keep his newly discovered faith long enough for deep roots to develop, he will discover a maturity that can provide a hidden reserve of strength for difficult times. True faithfulness is not determined by the ebb and flow of a human's passing moods and feelings. Neither is it based upon circumstances, for God never taught carnal security. Nor is it founded upon the faithfulness of other people. How many times do we hear someone offer the waywardness of others as the excuse for his own disobedience to God's commands. A Christian does not shift the responsibility of his misconduct to someone else.

When a Christian has matured, his word is completely reliable. When he says he will do something, the matter is settled. He will do it if humanly possible. Not only his words but also his actions are reliable. Whenever the church assembles for worship, there is never any question about his being there. He will assemble with the saints regardless of headaches, sniffles or visiting relatives. When he is absent, everyone knows that it was impossible for him to come. When the elders ask such a person to perform a task—any task, regardless of how menial it might be—the job will be done. The Christian with the trait of faithfulness may not be ostentatious in his service; but he loyally continues, day in and day out, year after year. Through the hardships of even an unbelieving mate, his devotion is unwavering. **Life is so daily.** I have learned not to worry about the big calamities in life. Somehow, someway, we can find strength to meet these trials and remain faithful. It is the everyday living which really taxes our faithfulness.

Suggestions for Class Use

Lesson Twelve

1. Discuss the various meanings of **pistis,** the original word for faith.
2. Cite Scriptures that depict these nuances in the meaning of **pistis:** trustworthiness, assurance, reliability.
3. Read Psalm 91 aloud in class. Cite a New Testament example of the fulfillment of Psalm 91:11, 12.
4. Is God's faithfulness contradicted by His waiting? How many times do we interpret His delay as a negative answer when He is saying, in effect, "It is not yet time, my child"?
5. Are God's promises unconditional? What is **our** part?
6. When was God's promise to Abraham fulfilled? How long did Noah have to wait to see God's Word come to pass? Do you think God would have saved Noah if he had not built the ark? How would **you** have felt during this period of waiting? How can the faithfulness of God and Noah be compared with ours? (1 Peter 3:20, 21)
7. Why could the Hebrews not enter the promised land immediately? (See Hebrews 3:19) According to Numbers 14:34, why were these people required to wander in the

wilderness for forty years?

8. In our everyday lives how does unbelief lead to disobedience?

9. What was wrong with the sacrifices mentioned in the first chapter of Malachi? What was the attitude of the people (Malachi 1:13)? How do we show this same attitude in offering the leftovers of our lives?

10. If you have access to the records of the congregation, check to determine how many of those who were converted in the past five years are still faithful to the Lord.

11. According to the parable of the soils in Matthew 13, why do young plants frequently die so soon? Compare this plant growth with the one mentioned in Psalm 1.

12. Divide the class into three groups to discuss the futility of basing our faithfulness upon (1) our human moods, (2) the circumstances of fortunes of life, and (3) the faithfulness of others. Let each group summarize its findings before the assembled class.

13. Cite personal examples of individual steadfastness and loyalty among Christians of your acquaintance.

14. List some ways unfaithfulness may be seen in our own lives.

THE FRUIT OF THE SPIRIT IS MEEKNESS AND TEMPERANCE

The eighth fruit of the Spirit is **prautes,** which is translated **meekness.** Our modern connotation of the word causes us to think of a Walter Mitty type character and to view with contempt a person possessing this quality. We often associate meekness with spinelessness—a lack of strength. Many modern translations use the word **gentleness.** But still the real meaning escapes us.

First, let's look at some negative aspects. Meekness is not the opposite of courage; it takes courage to be meek. Neither is it false modesty nor a depreciation of self. While God's creatures are not to be preoccupied with themselves, He does expect them to have a healthy self-evaluation. After all, He loved us so much that He gave His only begotten son for our salvation (John 3:16). Not only is man more important than sheep (Matthew 12:12), he is placed just beneath the angels in importance (Psalm 8:5; Hebrews 2:7-9) and made in the image of God Himself (Genesis 1:26, 27). True meekness does not demand that a person be servile. Neither is such a quality a cowardly retreat from that which is right just to avoid conflict.

Earlier Greek literature used **prautes** to denote qualities of mildness, gentleness and meekness in dealing with others. The word (or the adjective **praus**) was used when referring to persons or things which possessed a soothing quality. Such phrases refer to words which will soothe a person when he is angry or resentful. They are also used in reference to an ointment that could soothe the pain of a wound. The adjective **praus** was used in describing an animal which had been tamed and brought under control. Plato used the word **prautes** in describing a watchdog who is vicious toward enemies and yet friendly toward those whom he knows and loves. Synonyms would be gentleness, humility, courtesy and consideration. Aristotle used this word as a quality of the man who is always angry at the right time and never at the wrong time. An unknown sage has observed that meekness is love at school. Strength and gentleness are perfectly combined in **prautes.**

The New Testament use of **prautes** carries an even deeper significance than the manner in which it was used in secular Greek. In inspired writings it probes more deeply than the outward behavior or dealings with one's fellowman. It is a submission of our wills to God as we accept His dealings with us as being for our ultimate good, whether we understand fully or not. Only the maturity of this fruit of the Spirit can enable anyone to accept injustices and wrongs in a spirit of meekness. If one's relationship toward God is right, this attitude will spill over in dealings with his fellowman.

OLD TESTAMENT

Naturally the Greek word **prautes** is not used in the Old Testament, but there are numerous passages in which a Hebrew word is translated similarly. "The meek shall eat and be satisfied" (Psalm 22:26). "But the meek shall inherit the earth" (Psalm 37:11). "The Lord lifteth up the meek" (Psalm 147:6).

Meekness implies control of anger and the tongue. Many Old Testament passages support this teaching. "He that is slow to wrath is of great understanding" (Proverbs 14:29). "A soft answer turneth away wrath" (Proverbs 15:1). "He that is slow to anger is better than the mighty; and he that ruleth his spirit than he that taketh a city" (Proverbs 16:32). "The discretion of a man deferreth his anger; and it is his glory to pass over a transgression'' (Proverbs 19:11). ''By long forbearing is a prince persuaded, and a soft tongue breaketh the bone'' (Proverbs 25:15). ''Wise men turn away wrath'' (Proverbs 29:8).

The pages of the Old Testament abound with living examples of meekness. Note Abraham's attitude toward his nephew in Genesis 13:8. Isaac displayed his father's meekness in dealing with the herdman of Gerar (Genesis 26:20-22). Gideon appeased the anger of the men of Ephraim by the manner in which he dealt with them in Judges 8:2, 3. Hannah could have justifiably lashed back at the false accusations of Eli, but this godly woman's soothing reply tempered the high priest's attitude as it is reflected in 1 Samuel 1:17. How many of us could have received Eliab's sarcastic rebuke in the manner in which David responded (1 Samuel 17:28, 29)?

Moses is the epitome of meekness: ''Now the man Moses was very meek, above all the men which were upon the face of the earth'' (Numbers 12:3). This praise is even more meaningful when one considers the context. The description came at a time when Miriam and Aaron were rebelling against the leadership of Moses.

Moses was not born with a meek character as is evidenced by his killing an Egyptian who had been beating an Israelite. The molding of Moses' character required forty years in the crucible of the desert of Midian as he learned that many battles are not won with might but by the strength of God. It was after years of relative solitude as a shepherd that Moses felt his inadequacy in leading God's people from Egypt (Exodus 3 and 4). The ordeal of appearing before Pharaoh, the ten plagues, crossing the Red Sea and years of leading a disgruntled people through a barren wilderness taught Moses the necessity of absolute trust and reliance upon God, which is the essence of meekness. No one could call this mighty leader of the Israelites a spineless, weak character. God's chosen one could be angry when the occasion justified such action, but he could also be submissive when God demanded it.

NEW TESTAMENT USES

Perhaps we can best get the **feel** of the way in which meekness is used in the New Testament by examining various passages.

Christ used the adjective form, **praus,** in the Beatitudes: "Blessed are the meek: for they shall inherit the earth" (Matthew 5:5). He used a form of the word when speaking of His own disposition: "Take my yoke upon you, and learn of me; for I am meek and lowly in heart: and ye shall find rest unto your souls" (Matthew 11:29). Matthew uses the reference from Zechariah 9:9 in the fifth verse of the twenty-first chapter: "Behold, thy King cometh unto thee, meek, and sitting upon an ass." In 1 Peter 3:4 the same word is used when speaking of the qualities of a Christian wife: ". . . even the ornament of a meek and quiet spirit."

The noun **prautes** is used in a number of instances by New Testament writers. Paul made reference to the meekness and gentleness of Christ in 2 Corinthians 10:1. The same writer urged Titus to teach meekness as a desired quality instead of speaking evil and being brawlers (Titus 3:2). God's elect are to display meekness as well as mercy, kindness, humbleness of mind and longsuffering (Colossians 3:12). Paul asked the Corinthians whether he should come to them with a rod or in love and in the spirit of meekness (1 Corinthians 4:21). The Galatians are given instructions for restoring a fallen brother: "Ye which are spiritual, restore such a one in the spirit of meekness" (Galatians 6:1). Instead of being contentious, the servant of the Lord is to be gentle and patient, instructing in meekness (2 Timothy 2:24, 25). James admonished the brethren to receive the engrafted word with meekness (James 1:21). Peter urged Christians to answer the religious questions of others with meekness and fear (1 Peter 3:15).

Christ is the supreme example of meekness in action as He suffered the humiliation and ordeals of the cross (2 Peter 2:21-24). Isaiah had prophesied that our Lord would not give the accusations of Pilate the dignity of a reply (Isaiah 53:7 and Matthew 27:14). It was the power of meekness which prompted Jesus to submit to His arrest when Judas had betrayed Him (Matthew 26:47-56). Our Lord could see beyond the natural inclination of revenge when He submitted to the will of the Father.

How often we humans think we must settle all wrongs and injustices and leave nothing to God. How contrary it is to our natures to bless those that persecute us (Romans 12:14), to do good to those who hate us and despitefully use us (Luke 6:27, 28). How difficult it is to turn the other cheek when we have been struck or to give even more than demanded in a law suit (Matthew 5:38-40). In fact, it is better for Christians to suffer wrong than to go to law against one another (1 Corinthians 6:7). Only this fruit of the Spirit could strengthen a child of God to the point that he could overcome the natural tendency to render evil for evil (1 Thessalonians 5:15). Only then can he rebuke without rancour, or be angry and sin not. Through this virtue our explosive passions are harnessed into the service of God. Like all other fruits, growth is impossible without proper planting and cultivating.

WORD STUDY OF **TEMPERANCE**

The final fruit of the Spirit is **enkrateia,** which is translated **temperance.** It means having a mastery of one's desires and impulses—self-control or the control of all sins of personal excess. The word itself does not imply any particular desire or impulse. The context must be relied upon to give specific meanings.

When we go to secular Greek, we find that the word was used as a virtue of an emperor who does not allow his personal interests to influence the government of his people. Plato defined the word as self-mastery or mastery of desires.

NEW TESTAMENT USES

The noun enkrateia is found in two other passages. When Felix had heard Paul, "he reasoned of righteousness, **temperance,** and judgment to come" and then sent Paul away (Acts 24:25). In 2 Peter 1:6 the same word is used in a similar list of Christian graces. Some have observed that **temperance** follows **knowledge** and must thus be learned.

The adjective, **enkrates**, which is translated **temperate**, is listed as a qualification of an elder in Titus 1:8.

The verb form, **enkrateuomai**, is rendered "is temperate" in 1 Corinthians 9:25 in reference to the rigid self-control of an athelete.

A different form of the same word is used in 1 Corinthians 7:9 when Paul speaks of self-control in sexual matters.

PRACTICAL APPLICATION

The Christian's life is not a monastic one. It does not necessitate a withdrawal from everyday life to prove one's self-control. Some things are strictly forbidden in the life of a child of God. Others are permissible but must not be done in excess. The Old Testament laws clearly delineated the boundaries of the Israelites, who lived under a rigid system of THOU SHALT and THOU SHALT NOT. In contrast, the permissive society of today urges few restraints but instead advocates that each one should be free to do "his own thing." The Perfect Law of Liberty is a balance between the two.

This seems to be the age of guided missiles and misguided men. We plan the course of missiles but let people do as they please. A missile would have a most difficult time reaching the moon if we gave no more direction to its course than we do to our lives. Such a permissive philosophy has permeated child-rearing principles and educational guidelines.

Rebellion against any form of restraint is not a new concept. During the days of the judges, "every man did that which was right in his own eyes" (Judges 17:6). The only way one can be truly happy is to be bound by the laws of God. "And ye shall know the truth, and the truth shall make you free" (John 8:32). "No man is free who is not master of himself" (Epictetus). We are free in the right channel. Humans are not structures but flowing rivers whose usefulness depends upon how they are channeled. This liquid power can be harnessed by dams to produce something beneficial; or its undisciplined, swirling waters can cause endless destruction when allowed to surge without restraint. "The man who masters himself through self-discipline never can be mastered by others" (Andrew Carnegie).

Paul had to keep his body under subjection to run the Christian race properly (1 Corinthians 9:27). Contrast this discipline with those who have no control over the desires of the body and whose God is their belly (Philippians 3:19). (That one hits a lot of us!) Paul exemplified self-control during his encounter with the high priest in Acts 23:1-5. The Sanhedrin had met under Roman order in a pretrial hearing to determine whether or not there was really a case against Paul. Since this apostle had not been proven guilty and was thus considered innocent, the command of Ananias to have Paul struck on the mouth was uncalled for. The defendant was justified in his calling the high priest a hypocrite, or "white-washed wall." When Paul realized that the speaker was the high priest, he immediately gained control of himself and apologized.

"He that hath no rule over his own spirit is like a city that is broken down, and without walls" (Proverbs 25:28). We become slaves to whatever overpowers us (2 Peter 2:19). Temperance, or self-control, makes a person such a master of himself that he is qualified to be the servant of others (1 Corinthians 9:19).

Christianity changes a person from within instead of restraining externally. Society may restrain thieves from stealing by placing them behind bars, but that could hardly be called self-control.

CONCLUSION

We know what self-control means. Most of us know the kind of person we would like to be. In our minds we have an image of a truly beautiful Christian personality—one whose life is a living symbol of love, joy, peace, patience, gentleness, goodness, faithfulness, meekness and temperance. Such a person does the right things at the right time. The right words seem to slip from his tongue. He is master of his emotions. And then we look at ourselves. Oh, me! We mean well and truly want to be different, but there are so many snares in the way. We become rushed and tired. When little Johnny or Susie walks across the freshly waxed floor, our response is not exactly the epitome of self-control. But somehow, someway, we keep on trying.

It seems that we go about the problem backward. Our efforts at self-control are just about as futile as tightly clamping a lid on a pan of boiling water. Adverse emotions are not controlled by outward or even conscious restraint. Mastery over self is a **fruit** of careful planting and cultivating. We try to harvest the fruit when we have never bothered to plant the right seeds nor to properly cultivate the soil. Sometimes we manage to get the seed into the ground, but we fail to keep the weeds out. Think about it: the right seeds—thoughts that are true, honest, just, pure, lovely and of good report (planted in a receptive mind with proper cultivation and weeding)—**will** produce the desired fruits of love, joy, peace, longsuffering, gentleness, goodness, faith, meekness and temperance. "For in due season we shall reap, if we faint not" (Galatians 6:9). True, it's a life-time struggle; but the effort can change us from caterpillars to butterflies.

There is a saying which condenses the essence of this entire work into a single sentence: **"Sow an action and you reap a habit; sow a habit and you reap a character; sow a character and you reap a destiny."**

Suggestions for Class Use

Lesson Thirteen

1. What is the modern connotation of **meekness?**
2. How did secular Greek use the word?
3. What is the teaching of the Old Testament concerning the quality of meekness?
4. Cite passages to support the proper control of anger and the tongue.
5. Assign each of these Bible characters to small discussion groups: Abraham, Isaac, Gideon and Hannah. Let each group determine in what manner the character under consideration displayed meekness and then report to the class.
6. Moses was described as the meekest man on the face of

the earth (Numbers 12:3).

(a) Contrast Moses' feeling of inadequacy at the time of
the burning bush (Exodus 3 and 4) with his attitude
forty years earlier when he killed an Egyptian who was
beating an Israelite. What had brought about this
change?

(b) How did Moses receive the murmurings of the Israelites
in these passages: Exodus 14:10-14; Exodus 15:22-26;
Exodus 16:4-8; Exodus 17:1-7; Numbers 12:1-16;
Numbers 16:1-50?

(c) How did Moses show his meekness (absolute trust
and reliance on God) when he was not permitted to
enter the promised land (Deuteronomy 34:1-6)?

7. In what sense will the meek inherit the earth (Matthew
5:5)?

8. How does Luke 9:46-48 show a lack of meekness? (This
attitude is especially regretable when the reader considers
that Christ had just tried to tell His disciples of His death
in verses 44 and 45.)

9. What is the context of 1 Peter 3:4 in which wives are
admonished to have a meek and quiet spirit? How could
meekness be instrumental in converting an unbelieving
husband?

10. Read aloud in class these New Testament passages and
comment on the use of **meekness:** 2 Corinthians 10:1;
Titus 3:2; Colossians 3:12; 1 Corinthians 4:21; 2 Timothy
2:24, 25; James 1:21; 1 Peter 3:15.

11. What does the spirit of meekness have to do with the
restoration of a fallen brother (Galatians 6:1)?

12. Read 1 Peter 2:21-24 aloud in class. From the class
members solicit details of the incident from the Gospels.
What happened to Christ's beard (Isaiah 50:6)? If you
had been placed in a similar experience, what would your
reaction have been?

13. How is the Christian to react to his natural inclination of
revenge when he has been wronged? (Note Romans 12:14;
Luke 6:27, 28; Matthew 5:38-40; 1 Corinthians 6:7;
1 Thessalonians 5:15.)

14. What is a simple meaning of **temperance?**

15. When Felix reasoned of **temperance,** why did he send Paul

away? (See Acts 24:25.)
16. Why is an elder to be temperate? (Titus 1:8)
17. What sort of self-control must an athlete possess? (1 Corinthians 9:25)
18. When we speak of controlling the desires of the body, what do we usually think about? What does the phrase "whose God is their belly" mean? (Philippians 3:19)
19. How many works of the flesh listed in Galatians 5:19-21 stem from lack of self-control?
20. Do you think Paul's actions were justified in Acts 23:1-5?
21. State your reasons for agreeing or disagreeing with this statement: a person must be master of himself before he can be qualified to be the servant of others. (See 1 Corinthians 9:19.)
22. Can adverse emotions be controlled effectively by outward or conscious restraint?
23. Have a class member summarize the main thought of this entire study. (Note the last paragraph.)

REFERENCE BOOKS

The Analytical Greek Lexicon. New York: Harper and Brothers.

Barclay, William. **The Letter to the Galatians.** Edinburgh, Scotland: The Saint Andrew Press, 1962.

Berry, George Ricker. **The Interlinear Literal Translation of the Greek New Testament.** Chicago: Wilcox and Follett Company, 1954.

Harris, Thomas A., M.D. **I'm OK—You're Okay.** New York, New York: Avon Books, 1969.

Lambert, Gussie. **Gleaning from Galatians.** Shreveport, Louisiana: Gussie Lambert Publications, 1960.

Maltz, Maxwell, M.D. **Psycho-Cybernetics.** Englewood Cliffs, N.J.: Prentice Hall, Inc. 1960.

Quell, Gottfried, and Stauffer, Ethelbert. **Love.** London, 1958.

Thayer, Joseph Henry, DD. **Thayer's Greek-English Lexicon of the New Testament.** Grand Rapids, Michigan: Associated Publishers and Authors, Inc., 1885.

Vine, W. E. **An Expository Dictionary of New Testament Words.** Westwood, New Jersey: Fleming H. Revell Company, 1966.

Wuest, Kenneth S. **Galatians in the Greek New Testament.** Grand Rapids, Michigan: William B. Eerdmans Publishing Company, 1956.